"Rachel M. Srubas weaves a rich fabric of spiritual and psychological wisdom, knitting the personal and communal, inward and outward, ordinary and profound. Each meditation sparkles with a vivid story and masterful metaphor. Her gift for overhearing the divine voice amplifying each Scripture often arrested me in my tracks. Every page is laced with word associations that break open fresh meaning. Over and over, her words led me to deep reflection and contemplative awareness. I didn't want this book to end. It is one I will return to often and gift to others."

—**MARJORIE THOMPSON**, author of *Soul Feast*

"During Lent, we recall Jesus' sojourn in the desert—a time for generosity, simplicity, and, most of all, prayer. Rachel Srubas's vivid meditations make the season come alive as she invites us into our own desert places where Christ meets us with a love that will transform our hearts."

—**CARL MCCOLMAN**, author of *Eternal Heart*
and *The Big Book of Christian Mysticism*

"Presbyterian minister and Benedictine oblate Rachel Srubas not only resides in the Sonoran Desert but also is immersed in desert spirituality. So, when you choose this desert dweller as your guide for this Lenten journey, you will get Scripture references, evocative stories, reflections, pauses, prayers, and Sabbath rest-stop experiences. You will savor the short Scriptures, hear what a divine voice might be saying, smile at the personal stories, and be lulled into contemplative repose when you dive deeply into Lent with *The Desert of Compassion: Devotions for the Lenten Journey*."

—**TERESA BLYTHE**, director of the Phoenix Center for
Spiritual Direction and author of *50 Ways to Pray*
and *Spiritual Direction 101*

"Rachel Srubas has transformed my experience of Lent, rearranging my expectations for this sacred season. 'Compassion flourishes' in the Lenten journey, she says. And here's what she means by that: Lent is a compassion practice–a grace-filled path of experiencing and enacting divine compassion for ourselves, others, and the world."

—**ANDREW DREITCER**, Professor of Spirituality and Codirector of the
Center for Engaged Compassion, Claremont School of Theology

The Desert of Compassion

Find digital resources for study,
worship, and sharing at
www.wjkbooks.com/DesertOfCompassion

The Desert of Compassion

Devotions for the Lenten Journey

Rachel M. Srubas

WESTMINSTER
JOHN KNOX PRESS
LOUISVILLE · KENTUCKY

First edition
Published by Westminster John Knox Press
Louisville, Kentucky

23 24 25 26 27 28 29 30 31 32—10 9 8 7 6 5 4 3 2 1

Unless otherwise indicated, Scripture quotations are from the New Revised Standard Version of the Bible, copyright © 1989 by the Division of Christian Education of the National Council of the Churches of Christ in the U.S.A., and are used by permission. Scripture quotations from the Inclusive Bible: The First Egalitarian Translation, copyright © 2007 by Priests for Equality, published in the United States of America by Rowman & Littlefield Publishers, Inc. Scripture quotations marked CEB are from the Common English Bible, copyright © 2011 Common English Bible, and are used by permission.

Book design by Sharon Adams
Cover design by Mary Ann Smith
Cover art: Silence of the Heart *by Sheila Mahoney Keefe.*
Used by permission.

Library of Congress Cataloging-in-Publication Data is on file
at the Library of Congress, Washington, DC.

ISBN-13: 978-0-664-26798-8

Most Westminster John Knox Press books are available at special quantity discounts when purchased in bulk by corporations, organizations, and special-interest groups. For more information, please e-mail SpecialSales@wjkbooks.com.

For Laura Munroe, Shirin McArthur,
and Brad Munroe—
desert dwellers, faithful friends,
creative keepers of the Word.

Contents

Week 2: Reach Out Your Hand

Connecting with people wounded by life makes compassion possible.

Week 3: Stay Awake with Me

Compassion requires distress tolerance, which practice strengthens.

Week 4: Your Whole Mind

Mindful awareness and thoughtful reflection foster wise compassion.

Week 5: Do Not Condemn
*Condemnation stymies grace, but compassion dismantles
shame and fosters healing.*

Holy Week: Do This and You Will Live
*Wherever wounded creatures may be found, compassion
takes action to alleviate suffering.*

Afterword
Through suffering and death, new life and compassion arise.

Orientation at the Trailhead

*W*elcome, traveler. You and I are about to embark on a journey through the Lenten desert with the compass of compassion in hand. To orient you toward the days ahead, I offer you here a few wayfinding words.

The reading for each weekday and Saturday of Lent begins with a Scripture passage relevant to the day's compassion-centered theme. An italicized message follows in which an imagined divine voice speaks. An ornamental break then suggests a meditative pause. The day's devotion goes on to explore a feature of Lent's inner and outer landscapes, concluding with a prayer. On each Sunday, a "Sabbath Rest Stop" introduces the coming week's compassion-focused theme and encourages you to devote part of the day to worshiping God with others. The book concludes where Lent reaches its culmination: three sacred days signifying God's encompassing compassion for all creation, made real in Jesus' death and resurrection.

If there's a spiritual journey more needful these days than the trek through life's hard places toward the sacred land of loving-kindness, I don't know what it might be. What I do know is this: I'm setting out on the wilderness way that points toward Easter's promise of mercy and wholeness for all. Our mutual companionship in Lent, yours and mine, could make the lonesome valley less so.

Lent's Early Days

Go to the Land That I Will Show You

Ash Wednesday

Go from Here

Now the LORD said to Abram, "Go from your country and your kindred and your father's house to the land that I will show you. I will make of you a great nation, and I will bless you, and make your name great, so that you will be a blessing."
—Genesis 12:1–2

Leave everything you know and everyone you love. Walk away from the land you live on, the language you speak, the relations who connect you to this place, the ancestors who anchor you in history. On the strength of nothing but my word, with nothing to go on but your faith in me, set out for a future you cannot imagine. I have great intentions for you and for people yet to be blessed through your trust in me. You can't prepare yourself for what I will do. You can only follow my voice.

There once lived a monk named Father Louis. In the heart of a century, at the heart of a country, in a monastery called Gethsemani, he was appointed master of scholastics. In this role he ministered to monks preparing for the priesthood. This was, he confessed in his private diary, a responsibility he had once feared would interfere with his single-hearted relationship with God. But six months into the work, he understood that "the care of souls can serve to lead one further into the desert." The desert, for all its severity and solitude, was the place where Father Louis, better known as Thomas Merton, felt summoned to go.

5

"What is my new desert?" he asked. "The name of it is compassion. There is no wilderness so terrible, so beautiful, so arid, and so fruitful as the wilderness of compassion. It is the only desert that will flourish like the lily."[1]

The desert, as Merton's words make evident, is a paradox, a place and a spiritual condition in which terror leads to beauty and aridity bears fruit. Compassion is such a desert. The "com" of compassion means "with" and "passion" means "suffer" but can also mean ardor, all-consuming love. Compassion is the human capacity to do what God does in Jesus: suffer with another out of deep, self-giving love and discover that through such suffering comes solace and—dare I say it?—even joy.

I call this book *The Desert of Compassion* because I am a follower of Jesus and the desert is the place where he went for forty days to fast, pray, and prepare for the life God intended him to live and give. Jesus' forty days of desertion and temptation led him to a compassionate ministry so fruitful it made water sweeten into wine, bent-over women stand upright, blind men see, and dying children live. Jesus loved and suffered with broken-backed, overlooked, written-off people. He entered, heart and soul, into the deserts where they struggled in exile, having been deemed useless and demonic by their own society. In reality, they were God's beloved people, inherently worthy and intended for blessing. Jesus could see this as no one else could until he spat in the dirt and smeared the muddy plaster of compassion on the unseeing eyes of the world. Even then, many still refused to recognize who Jesus was and what he meant.

He means even now to lead you into the desert of compassion, the place within you where hurt gives rise to hope and devastation births the desire for redemption. You don't want to go there on your own, and why would you? Why would you want to go alone into that hospital room, that bad memory, that miserable meeting, that place of captivity, that land where people's lives are taken? The pain, the scary scenery, the struggle that summons you to the desert appears devoid of mercy and goodness.

And here is the holy dilemma. The only way to get to the goodness of God, to make it to the mercy that saves this world, is to move headlong into hardship and through it. I am not—let me hasten to say—urging you to go looking needlessly for trouble. I am saying that to be human is to hurt, sometimes very badly. Yet the One who made us, the Creator whom Jesus called *Abba*, does not intend hardship to be a dead end but a point of departure toward a life so transformed it can only be called new.

Ash Wednesday is a day of departure, and Lent is a long walk down a desert path. Deceptive signs along the way may announce "NO OUTLET." But the follower of Jesus in the desert suspects that Jesus knows a truth the signs don't tell, and presses on, fear be damned. In this journey through Lent, I offer to walk with you day by day. I reflect on some old Scripture stories and on some newer situations that echo the gospel calling us to love God, ourselves, and others with abandon. In so doing, we will surely die and rise.

Rising sounds good. It's the dying we dread. It's the suffering—our own and other people's—that we often try to circumvent, and that gets us nowhere. So, in these pages I also offer prayers to help you get to the land that God will show you. Take this book with you as you set out on your desert pilgrimage toward a compassionate life. Along the way, may your heart be broken open in blessing.

God of dust and ashes, of departures and paradox,
why did you let Jesus hurt and die like us?
Lead me to the desert where I may come to understand.
Make me brave enough to feel the heat of the day,
the hungers of my body, the beat of my heart,
and your love for all mortal flesh.
Amen.

First Thursday of Lent

The Roundabout Way

> When Pharaoh let the people go, God did not lead them by way of the land of the Philistines, although that was nearer; for God thought, "If the people face war, they may change their minds and return to Egypt." So God led the people by the roundabout way of the wilderness toward the Red Sea. The Israelites went up out of the land of Egypt prepared for battle."
> —Exodus 13:17–18

A route may appear to include few detours and delays. But there are no shortcuts. The seeming fast track will force you to backtrack and consume the time you meant to save. The wilderness path to the eventually parted Red Sea wends through hard terrain because the only way home is the long way. You can neither rush it nor go it alone. Alone, you'll get lost in a hurry. With me, you'll reach your destination in due time.

Lent's opening day is behind you. No one's forehead bears an ashy smudge today. Clean-faced, forge ahead into this season with only a general sense of direction. You're bound for Easter, weeks away.

The original, literal meaning of the English word "Lent" is to lengthen. In the Northern Hemisphere, as Earth emerges slowly from winter's dark, the daylight hours lengthen and natural signs of new life appear. Trees sprout tender green leaves. Infant birds break free from their shells, blessedly oblivious to climate change. They know only that it's spring, it's their birthday, and they're hungry.

8

Maybe you're hungry, too, for light or renewal. Perhaps you have a goal in mind for Lent, something you'd like to get out of this season or accomplish by Easter Sunday. Hope and the hunger for transformation are good. Notice them. Feel their creative energy urging you forward from within. And hold humbly the notion that you can know where you're going or how long it will take you to get there. Make plans, but remember, God's purposes and pace can't be predicted or controlled. You can guess, but you can't foretell the changes you'll go through. Or will the changes go through you? Time will tell, but how much time? You'll grow into knowing, slowly. Revelation can't be hustled.

A few years into our marriage, when we were graduate students in our hometown, Chicago, my husband (a little like Abram called to go from his country and kindred) ventured to a desert neither of us knew, for a job interview. During that visit to faraway Tucson, Arizona, Ken bought me a necklace. He gave it to me after he learned he'd landed the job. At the end of a black silken cord hung a rectangular silver locket that opened like a book. Inside, a paper strip, accordion-folded, could be unfurled to reveal a topographic design and this handwritten message: "The map is not the territory." The necklace was Ken's way of saying, "Come away with me on a journey into the desert. I don't know where it will take us, but together, we'll find out."

In August, like broke tenants skipping out on the rent (we weren't), we emptied our apartment and left town after dark, during the coolest available hours. A heatwave was bearing down on the states we'd have to drive through, our car lacked an air conditioner, and we would be transporting two housecats more stressed-out than we were. We had never been enslaved—far from it. But maybe we felt a little like the liberated Israelites who followed God by the roundabout way, prepared for battle. We were armed only with the belief that together, by faith, we would get through this unmapped stretch of our life and be led where we needed to go.

Deep in Oklahoma, we wearily scanned the highway exits for someplace open at that ungodly hour where we could get caffeine and food. There it was, squat and glowing at the edge of an unlit frontage road—a Waffle House with a burned-out "W" on its otherwise luminous sign. Ken said aloud what we both were thinking: "It's an Awful House."

When the only way station in sight is an Awful House serving up hot, brown water and calling it "coffee," you know you've entered the wilderness. We sat at a table among the smattering of truckers. Fatigue, grief, and fear waged war on my heart. I felt tempted to hitch a ride back to the place I'd always called home. My sister and her then-little boys had thrown us a send-off party. They'd baked us a cake decorated to look like a desert, with make-believe snakes slithering through cinnamon-sugar sands. That cake tasted sweeter than the tepid waffle in front of me now. But hadn't God provided this waffle? Isn't a meal, however measly, eaten in the middle of a long, hard journey, a gift? I gave thanks for my breakfast and decided not to turn back.

It's not that gratitude eliminates grief, nor that prayer cancels fear. The roundabout trip through your life's wilderness will make you aware of how sad and scared you are. Along the way, you will pause, exhausted, and feel it all: the loss of your familiars, the doubts about where on earth you're heading and why. It may seem you're getting nowhere. Sometimes you'll glimpse your goal but realize no direct path will take you to it. You'll have no choice but to take the circuitous route.

Your body may help you understand this if you walk a sacred labyrinth during Lent. A labyrinth symbolizes the roundabout way of the wilderness. Whether it's tiled into a cathedral floor, mown into a lawn, or painted onto a canvas mat, a labyrinth's circuits are meant to be walked in slow, prayerful circles not unlike those the Israelites walked toward the Red Sea. They may have asked the same questions you'll ask: Why, the closer you get to its end, does the journey become more convoluted? What's the point? The point is the path itself, and you, following it on sheer faith.

God of the journey, you meet me coming and going.
Show me, one step at a time, the path I'm meant to follow.
Keep me from getting ahead of myself.
Walk beside me, and when I get tired,
lead me to places where I can be fed and bed down.
Watch over the interstate saints, the truckers and short-order cooks,
gas station cashiers and all whose labors make navigable
the dark, roundabout way.
Amen.

First Friday of Lent

The Wellspring of Everyone's Well-Being

But Sarah saw the son of Hagar the Egyptian, whom she had borne to Abraham, playing with her son Isaac. So she said to Abraham, "Cast out this slave woman with her son; for the son of this slave woman shall not inherit along with my son Isaac." . . . So Abraham rose early in the morning, and took bread and a skin of water, and gave it to Hagar, putting it on her shoulder, along with the child, and sent her away. And she departed, and wandered about in the wilderness of Beer-sheba.

—Genesis 21: 9–10, 14

To the one whose blessedness turned to bitter laughter, I offer the mercy she refused to show her neighbor. The one who divided his own heart, reducing to rivals those to whom he portioned out its broken pieces, I love wholeheartedly, nevertheless. The forsaken ones whose masters cast them into the wilderness, I meet in the places of their depletion, to dig for them a freshwater well. And they drink.

In Lent, you enter the season of repentance. You follow the voice that calls through the prophet Joel, "Return to me with all your heart" (2:12). To repent is to return to God with your heart wide open, so that over time, you may be turned by mercy into a truer version of yourself: healed, uncorrupted, and kind.

The return trip to God, as yesterday's reflection on the roundabout wilderness way pointed out, is winding and long. It's the journey of a lifetime; it takes you your whole life to make it. As every Sunday is a little Easter that celebrates the resurrection no single day can contain, so every Lent is a little lifetime. This Lent is one leg in your life-long trip toward transformative compassion.

By the vulnerable way of Lenten repentance, you'll make your way back to God. Your task in this season is to seek, day by day and prayer by prayer, the One who calls you to return. Part of your spiritual work is to ask yourself, with utmost gentleness and courage, *Why did you leave? Who drove you out? Where did you go? What will it take to restore you?* The answers aren't likely to come fast. When they do eventually come, listen long and well, as the One to whom you pray listens to you. Allow time for silence. It may convey insights you can't come by otherwise.

Were you to ask Abram and Sarai, "Why did you leave? Who drove you out? Where did you go?" before their fortunes increased and their names were altered, they would say they left their ancestral homeland because the Lord dispatched them to Canaan, promising through them to bless all families of the earth. But ask the same questions of Hagar, and she could tell you the story of her sexual enslavement. When the son Hagar bore to Abram at Sarai's behest posed an emotional and economic threat to the covenantal couple's family, they colluded to drive Hagar and Ishmael to their deaths in the Negev Desert. Hagar laid her little boy under the shade of a bush, sat a bow-shot's distance from him, and prayed he wouldn't die of thirst.

Water is life. Opening her eyes, Hagar found a water well she hadn't seen before. The Lord of life turns up at wells where women weep and work and wait for salvation, their own and their children's. Hagar filled her bottle and gave Ishmael a saving drink. The two of them had committed no sin. They returned to the Lord not by the repentant way of confession and amends, but by a fount of blessing that led them back to life.

Abraham and Sarah, beneficiaries of a culture of enslavement, did not seem to see any need to repent of the harm they had done to Hagar and son. Today, however, white-privileged readers of their story may be prompted to ask, what harm has our social group's undeserved supremacy done to minoritized people? What reparations have we left unmade?

Readers in communities of color may see themselves, their families, cultures, and histories in Hagar's oppression and her son's helpless dependence. Black and brown readers may repent by way of social resistance, refusing to drink any longer from their oppressors' wells, returning to God by reclaiming stolen sacred lands, languages, and rights. Where communal memories of enslavement and exile reverberate as truthfully as Hagar's and Ishmael's story reverberates now, repentance, in Lent or any season, can't remain purely private.

Nothing, not even your spirituality, is yours alone. From your smallest gesture to your grandest intention, you live your life alongside all other creatures. From the water you drink to the plumber who fixes your sink, everything and everyone exists in a network of creation and culture. The innermost shifts you make to turn prayerfully Godward cause ripples that reach your neighbors. Remember them as you seek to make your way back to God.

Hearing others' stories, letting their struggles infuse your awareness, can cause you to care about people you may never personally know, whose humanity intersects with yours all the same. Compassionate openness on your part can influence not only how you feel but also how you vote, the books you read, the products you purchase. Openness toward others can advance your becoming the wholehearted person God calls you to be.

Your name is on God's lips. Today, whether you identify with Hagar and Ishmael in their desertion by powerful people, or, like Sarah and Abraham, you possess the power to force your will on others, you are called to turn toward the wellspring of everyone's well-being. Drink deep and come clean in waters that restore the rejected and carry their abandoners to justice with mercy. Return to the One who forsakes no one.

How have I forsaken you, my God?
Lead me to listen in silence
for your guidance. Teach me to listen
to people pushed to their limits,
whose exploiters have deserted them.
Let your compassion for rejected children and women
teach a better way than exploitation.
Finder of wanderers, call us all back to the well
where your restorative waters flow.
Amen.

First Saturday of Lent

Be Found in Solitude

Great crowds came to him, bringing with them the lame, the maimed, the blind, the mute, and many others. They put them at his feet, and he cured them, so that the crowd was amazed when they saw the mute speaking, the maimed whole, the lame walking, and the blind seeing. And they praised the God of Israel. Then Jesus called his disciples to him and said, "I have compassion for the crowd, because they have been with me now for three days and have nothing to eat; and I do not want to send them away hungry, for they might faint on the way." The disciples said to him, "Where are we to get enough bread in the desert to feed so great a crowd?"

—Matthew 15:30–33

When the weak and the strong rely on one another, the web of interdependence shines. Fortunate people taste their own hunger. Mercy nourishes depleted caregivers and equally strengthens the ones they support. In the desert of my compassion, there is bread enough for all.

"We're being 'californicated'!" So claim some Phoenicians, Tucsonans, and other desert dwellers of Arizona, where I live. *Californication* conveys a bitter whiff of territoriality—maybe even xenophobia. But the trends reflected in the term don't lie. At the time of this book's publication, the most recent available data on gross domestic migration showed "California contributed by far the most migrants to Arizona."[1]

I'm a migrant, myself, from Illinois, one of the top ten states from which people relocate to Arizona. I've got no business resenting anyone who moves to this desert from someplace else. But as increasing numbers of people have migrated to the Southwest, desert sprawl, "low-density, haphazard development spiraling outward from urban centers," has increased, damaging ecological and social environments.[2] It's a hazardous thing to overdevelop and crowd the desert, a landscape naturally arid, hot, and fragile.

Desert crowding is not a new phenomenon. As long ago as the year 360 CE, a Christian leader named Athanasius of Alexandria described the migration of contemplative Christians into the stark Egyptian wilderness: "The desert was made a city by monks who left their own people, and enrolled themselves for citizenship in the Heavens."[3] Although far smaller than a sprawling, desert metropolis such as Riyadh, Saudi Arabia (which has experienced massive population growth in recent decades), the fourth century "city" founded by monastic men and women points to the desert's spiritual allure. Its austere terrain attracts some seekers of a deeper inner life than they find in populous areas. But mass migration to the desert overbuilds its simplicity and crowds out its serenity.

In roughly the same time and place that Athanasius of Alexandria described the monastic desert city, a contemplative Egyptian woman named Syncletica, who served as a spiritual director to other women, came to be revered as a Desert Mother. Syncletica honored varying human temperaments and spiritual styles. "Each person should have confidence in his own disposition," she said. Syncletica prized the solitude that the physical desert encouraged, but acknowledged that the spiritual desert is an internal dwelling place where anyone may abide: "Many people, then, have found salvation in a city while imagining the conditions of a desert. . . . It is possible for one who is in a group to be alone in thought."[4]

If you feel called to the contemplative path of simplicity, prayerfulness, and reflection, you can pursue it wherever you are. A natural desert's wide earthen stretches and wind-sculpted rock formations may move you to reflect on the beautiful brevity of your life. But landscape alone can't make or break your spirituality. Syncletica urges people to venture in solitude into their interior desert, the silent center of the self where the Christ of compassion makes the maimed whole and feeds hungering souls.

This Lent, if you're aching for stillness, understanding, rest, or personal healing, it's because you're being sought. Your longing and unease are leading you to look for God, who is seeking to transform your hurts and yearnings into your wholeness and fulfillment. Jesus said of himself that he "came to seek out and to save the lost" (Luke 19:10). In the hymn "Amazing Grace," Englishman John Newton's phrase, "I once was lost," expresses the sense of spiritual desertion that drives people to look for God, who is never missing but is frequently missed. Once the lost seeker feels the breakthrough of divine compassion, the lyrical cry becomes, "But now I'm found."[5]

Like the undernourished crowd seeking Jesus' help for hurting loved ones, "found" people are fed. Folks who have never suffered from insufficient nutrition can experience spiritual hunger. A lack of love or a relentlessly crowded calendar can famish the soul. The communion needed then, according to Syncletica, is prayerful time alone.

The desert is intrinsic to everyone. You carry your desert inside you. Go there in solitude. In time you'll be fed by the Holy One who locates the lost and nourishes the hungry in the desert.

When I turn to you, thoughts crowd my solitude.
Distractions demand the attention I intend for you alone.
I'm lost and lacking the bread of your silence.
Come, find me. I'll wait.
Amen.

Week 1

Remove the Heart of Stone

Sabbath Rest Stop

It's Sunday, the Christian Sabbath, the Lord's Day. You've begun your Lenten journey through the desert of compassion. You'll continue in the week ahead to discover what it is to trek and sometimes stumble into foreboding terrain where liberating truths can be known and treasures of meaning can be unearthed.

The desert is available to you regardless of your local climate. Although I make my home in an actual desert, I spent over three decades living in wet, windy, sometimes snowbound Chicago. I appreciate Indiana-based writer Susan Yanos's article, "The Midwestern Winter as Spiritual Desert." Writing during the months after the death of her sister, Yanos speaks of the human heart in Hebrew biblical terms as "the self at its deepest level." She likens bleak, freezing winter to the spiritual desert through which, as the prophet Isaiah declares, a highway for the Lord must be made straight (40:3). "I've learned if I undergo the desert experience involuntarily, it can crush me," writes Yanos. "If voluntarily, it can be liberating. Giving the heart, my dearest treasure even though frozen and closed, is the voluntary acceptance of the desert."[1]

"Frozen" and "closed" are Midwestern winter names for the spiritual condition called hard-heartedness. Even in hard-frozen condition, the heart is the "dearest treasure" you can give. Acceptance makes the spiritual desert navigable and makes the difference between a freeing and a crushing experience. Accepting that life will inevitably lead you at times through the desert will foster your compassion toward struggling people, including yourself. Refusing to accept the desert as part of your life experience will only intensify its crushing effect on you. Maybe you've already learned the hard way this lesson of desert-acceptance.

The heartfelt way through the desert of compassion will be the theme of this week's reflections. Informing Monday through Saturday's readings will be a daunting-yet-divine promise: "I will remove the heart of stone from their flesh" (Ezek. 11:19). My own life has taught me that my wholeness in God depends on my accepting the tough, transformative replacement of my hard-hearted ways with flesh-hearted wisdom.

Sometimes I resist being transformed because changing requires me to do the difficult, vulnerable work of acknowledging loss, feeling distress, and facing uncertainty. But these don't crush me like the fruitless effort to avoid them does. When I acknowledge a loss, endure the distress it causes, turn toward an unknown future, and give thanks that I've come this far by faith, I find that, by God, there's a stretch of desert behind me. I've crossed it. And I'm pressing on.

There will be desert stretches ahead, but I've learned a little more than I understood before about getting through the desert alive and grateful. And now my heart, my inmost self, feels keenly for anyone else crossing a literal or figurative desert. The experience of feeling for other desert travelers tells me compassion is active within me. This means God is at work.

Feeling fully the sensual, emotional reality of your life means your inmost self, perhaps numbed and long hidden under a stony crust, is awakening. You are meant to emerge, live, move, and have your being in the One determined to soften hardened hearts. Today, participate if you can in a worship gathering that helps you, as the Holy Communion liturgy puts it, "lift up your heart to the Lord." Then, beginning with tomorrow's reflection, spend a week exploring the terrain of human feeling where, despite barren and arid conditions, your compassion for yourself and others can take deeper root and grow stronger.

Monday of Week 1

Feel Your Way

Thus says the Lord GOD: Though I removed them far away among the nations, and though I scattered them among the countries, yet I have been a sanctuary to them for a little while in the countries where they have gone. . . . I will give them one heart, and put a new spirit within them; I will remove the heart of stone from their flesh and give them a heart of flesh, so that they may follow my statutes and keep my ordinances and obey them. Then they shall be my people, and I will be their God.

—Ezekiel 11:16, 19–20

I am the sanctuary of exiles. With a love that seeks the scattered and gathers the shattered, I humanize petrified hearts and make them wholly capable of loving me in return. Devote yourself to well-being, your own as much as others'. Let loving-kindness be your practice. Let me be your God.

I once gave a talk to a roomful of spiritual seekers who generally weren't churchgoers. I spoke about personal transformation—"being changed by God," as I put it, particularly the process of becoming more compassionate. I offered a definition of compassion based on the word's Latin origins: *com* means *together with* and *passio* means *suffering*. "To have compassion," I told the gathered people, "is to *suffer with* someone."

After the talk, a man I guessed to be in his late seventies introduced

21

himself to me as a former Jesuit. (Jesuits are an order of Roman Catholic priests and brothers founded by Ignatius of Loyola and his companions in 1540. They seek God in all things and emphasize higher education.) The man suggested I broaden my definition of compassion. "It's more than suffer with," he said, "if you think of the Greek word pathos that the Latin *passio* is based on. It's passion. It's feeling! To have compassion is to feel with. I like that better than suffer with, don't you? It's not so dreary and martyrish."

I noticed my face growing warm, my breathing quickening slightly. I felt corrected and a little embarrassed, mansplained to and mildly annoyed, yet obligated to be a gracious guest presenter, willing to learn from people's feedback. "I like that, too," I said, half-truthfully. I was both considering the man's perspective and managing my response to him. It took me a while before I could genuinely appreciate the fact that because passion does mean feeling, compassion can mean more than solidarity in suffering. It can connote an openheartedness toward others in which there's room for a range and evolution of emotions, from confidence to irritation to curiosity to gratitude.

What the ex-priest called "dreary and martyrish," a psychological counselor might call "codependence." This term, widely used among addiction-recovery practitioners, is rooted in the work of Karen Horney, the first feminist psychoanalyst. In the early 1940s, Horney theorized that some people compulsively move toward those who are hurting and needy, ostensibly to offer help. The helpers' unacknowledged motivation, however, is to gain affection and approval for their selfless behavior. Commonly, the partners of chemically dependent people are co-dependent, unable to experience their inherent worth and therefore dependent for validation on the addicts they approach, rescue, and enable. Codependence is a dreary, martyrish cycle, not a compassionate partnership but a bond based on mutually perpetuated suffering.

The bond can and must be broken for healthy compassion to become possible. As the prophet Ezekiel puts it, a "heart of stone" can be broken open and transformed by God, the unseen change agent. People with a "heart of flesh" have been freed from the petrifying bondage of shame. No longer convinced of their unworthiness nor driven to reinforce it through emotional martyrdom, flesh-hearted people know they are wholly God's people. Their sense of sacred worth makes them capable of compassion for themselves and others.

Historically, Lent was heavy on guilt and light on, well, light. Ignatius of Loyola left a spiritual legacy adaptable by people who need to lighten up their Lent. In *Spiritual Exercises*, Ignatius wrote about "consolations and desolations," emotional experiences that help you tell whether you've drawn close to God or become distant. The more consoled you feel, the more hopeful, faithful, giving, joyous, and serene, the closer you've come to God. Conversely, the more disturbed, agitated, tempted, and underconfident you feel, the lazier, lukewarm, and sadder your inner state, the more you need the people and practices that lighten your load and bring you back to God.

In Ezekiel's words, you need a heart of flesh. Feel your feelings in your muscles, bones, and breath. Consider the messages your bodily sensed emotions send you. If you're happy and you know it, thank your God. If you're feeling deserted or stonehearted, you're not spiritually deficient, but you are suffering desolation for some reason, so be kind to yourself. Do the things you love that bring you back to life. Be consoled by God's message, spoken about people in exile: "Though I removed them far away. . . yet I have been a sanctuary to them."

Sanctuary of all flesh,
take away the stone I've turned to inside.
I'll take in the gift of your new spirit
and let go the breath I need no longer hold.
Amen.

Tuesday of Week 1

Live with Feeling

> Again he entered the synagogue, and a man was there who had a withered hand. They watched him to see whether he would cure him on the sabbath, so that they might accuse him. And he said to the man who had the withered hand, "Come forward." Then he said to them, "Is it lawful to do good or to do harm on the sabbath, to save life or to kill?" But they were silent. He looked around at them with anger; he was grieved at their hardness of heart and said to the man, "Stretch out your hand." He stretched it out, and his hand was restored. The Pharisees went out and immediately conspired with the Herodians against him, how to destroy him.
>
> —Mark 3:1–7

Come forward, reach out. Your restoration is at hand. Take hold of the life you've been unable to grasp until today. Wave good-bye to failed silencers whose righteous hearts have turned to marble. Threatened by goodness they can't perfect, they scheme to eliminate mercy they don't realize they need. Eventually, it will find them because I withhold compassion from no one.

The phone rang around nine that night. My mother, advanced in age, had fallen at home. She'd struck her head on a table. Her scalp was bleeding and the bleeding wouldn't stop.

The quiet evening blurred into a rush of first responses—call 911,

24

leave the house, push toward the green lights, meet her at the ER—
and wait.

And wait. In the chill, glaring desert that is a hospital emergency
room.

Her silver hair turned a matted, sticky auburn as she lay on a gur-
ney under fluorescent lights. The staffers seemed to amble through
their tasks, triaging nothing. If they'd determined there was no immi-
nent danger to my mother's life, they hadn't said so.

A few hours, several sutures, and a bandage turban later, my mother
was laying her tender (and apparently tough) head on her own pillow,
in her own bed. The bloodied carpet in her bedroom smelled of iron.
Exhausted, I lay blinking in the dark guestroom, wheezing from the
cat hair embedded in the blanket covering me. My brain reran the ER
scene and my body surged with anger at the slowpoke staffers. Grief
and relief mingled within me at the thought of my mother in the next
room, small and safe in her own bed, sleeping off her hard knock.
Eventually, I slipped into a shallow sleep that ended abruptly at day-
break when one of her cats jumped on me, meowing for breakfast.

After the cats ate, we got ourselves carryout pancakes. We rented a
cumbersome wet/dry vacuum cleaner for the stained bedroom carpet.
Life crept forward. My mother healed. Eventually, a doctor snipped
out the sutures and gave her the medical scissors to keep. She used
purple shampoo and her hair curved and shone once again, the color
of sunlit snowdrifts.

If my former houseplants could talk, they'd tell you that unlike
Jesus, I cannot restore what has withered. Neither can you because
you, like me, are merely, yet dearly, human. If you—God forbid—
should gash your head, you'd bleed, probably profusely. If someone
you loved were bleeding, you might get mad at the slackers who could
help her but seemed unduly slow to do so. Your anger would make
you, as mine made me, rather Christlike. Jesus got good and angry at
the rulebound bystanders who let a man suffer unattended while they
scrutinized Jesus, the only one who bothered to help.

Beneath Jesus' anger lay grief—a broken rock from which water
flows like tears, like mine flowed when I lay in the guestroom bed,
flooded with gladness that my mother hadn't been more seriously
injured, yet overcome with sadness that she'd fallen and hit her head
in the first place. Sorrowing at this fallible human condition of ours,

I felt how fragile we all are, how withered we become, how tenderized and scarred our hearts, how hardened.

The Greek word for the "hardness" of heart that grieved Jesus is also the name of a marble called *pōros*. Of this, archaeologist Richard Wycherley wrote, "Marble . . . is a limestone miraculously metamorphosed by titanic heat and pressure into its characteristic crystalline structure, thus forming in the body of the earth . . . poroi, callouses or nodules."[1]

Pressure-and-heat-hardened stones make for a sturdy temple. But they make for a heart incapable of compassion. Those who conspired to destroy Jesus after he healed a man on the Sabbath also needed healing—for their hard-heartedness. They neither recognized this need nor sought help for themselves. God knows what social pressures, what political heat, had borne down on them, turning them, effectively, to stone.

The ER staffers, nonplussed in their rubber clogs and uniform scrubs, may have become trauma-hardened long before my mother and I encountered them. Demeanors that looked stonehearted to me may have appeared professionally serene to other observers. After all, a "bleeding heart" staffer won't survive long in the ER. Neither, however, should someone so emotionally sealed as to lack empathy.

The art of the heart involves both feeling and regulating emotions. Sometimes, people become hard-hearted rather than work to develop emotional fluency. A structural key to emotional fluency—the capacity to experience, recognize, and manage emotions—lies within that marble word, *pōros*. A heart of *pōros* isn't only hard, it's also porous. Deep in its crystalline being, it has permeable pores. Water, blood, anger, grief, love, and mercy can flow in and out. Even a Pharisee with cardiac calluses was originally created to receive and give compassion. With vulnerability, holy help, and practice, hard-hearted people can learn to live with feeling, which makes compassion possible.

To nurses and doctors, attendants and orderlies
laboring far from the hôtel-Dieu,
the "hostel of God" that a hospital once was;
to patients identified only by the birthdates on their wristbands;
to places where efficiency outstrips mercy,
Holy Healer, let your compassion come.
Amen.

Wednesday of Week 1

Desert Struggle

In those days Jesus came from Nazareth of Galilee and was baptized by John in the Jordan. And just as he was coming up out of the water, he saw the heavens torn apart and the Spirit descending like a dove on him. And a voice came from heaven, "You are my Son, the Beloved; with you I am well pleased." And the Spirit immediately drove him out into the wilderness. He was in the wilderness forty days, tempted by Satan; and he was with the wild beasts; and the angels waited on him.

—Mark 1:9–13

My Spirit breaks free of the ripped-open heavens and dives down into your life. Precise and fearless in her descent, she is not violent, but neither is she delicate. With an elegant economy of wing beats, she alights to make you know I'm pleased to call you my beloved child. Yet she also sends you far from your customary comforts into wild places. She is the reason you'll dare to face your fears and endure the trials of your desert season. She will see you through to your new, true self, now burgeoning.

In church on a Sunday in Lent, when you hear (perhaps for the fortieth or four hundredth time) the story of Jesus tempted in the wilderness, the verses may sound so familiar, the outcome so predictable, that the gravity and hope of the situation may elude you. If your heart feels hardened against the story of Jesus' desert struggle, read your daily newsfeed alongside the Gospel. Let stories of injustice, poverty, hunger, addiction, and violence infiltrate your prayers. Remember there is a greater good, a greater God at work than all other powers. By the same Spirit who drove Jesus into the desert and empowered him to resist the malevolent tempter, you are called to live your life in the service of this greater God. Lent is a reminder of your calling.

The Latin name for Lent, *quadrigesima*, means fortieth. Lent's length (forty days plus the six Sundays between Ash Wednesday and Easter) is patterned after the duration of Jesus' temptation in the desert. In biblical terms, the number forty means, roughly speaking, a long time. Consider this alongside Lent's original definition: to lengthen. Lent's forty (or forty-six) days are meant to run long and test your spiritual endurance. Lent will urge you to stick with your spiritual disciplines and be sustained by them, especially when forty days seem like forever.

What can it mean to be sustained by discipline? How can a spiritual practice like Lenten fasting or almsgiving sustain you when it involves abstaining from certain consumables or relinquishing a portion of your goods? Fasting would seem to leave you depleted and weak.

For physical and mental health reasons, some people should not engage in a dietary fast, and no one should undertake a fast carelessly or excessively. But people who are bodily and spiritually prepared to go without food for a limited period can endure the discomfort of a grumbling stomach and experience, through fasting, heightened awareness of their daily dependence on God's provisions, their habitual overconsumption of unneeded calories, and the hunger that afflicts millions of people. The rich fruits of going without food can be these: increased gratitude to God, consciousness of excess, and a heart broken open in compassion for people made poor. Abstinence from food can make the heart grow hungrier for justice.

Mark's Gospel, with its spare narrative, doesn't state that Jesus went without food during his desert sojourn. However, according to Matthew (4:2) and Luke (4:2), Jesus fasted for forty days and then was famished. The real struggle began when Jesus was weak with hunger, possibly delirious. I don't even like to skip lunch, much less six weeks of meals. Imagine how vulnerable and how gaunt Jesus must have been when, as all three Gospels attest, he confronted the alluring, death-dealing power of evil in the form of a being called Satan.

Temptation of the compelling, destructive magnitude that Jesus faced makes laughable such Lenten "fasts" as giving up chocolate—unless chocolate happens to be your gateway drug to a full-blown sugar binge and a diabetic coma. As the daughter of an alcoholic father (now deceased), I know about addiction, the baffling, cunning, powerful force of compulsive overconsumption. I know that the sinister presence who showed up at Jesus' moment of weakness, tempting him to do the very things that would destroy him, can be compared to addiction's hold on a human life.

For some people, this will be the Lent when they finally admit they're powerless over alcohol or drugs and seek help to begin down the path of sobriety. Your Lenten practices may be that pivotal, or they may be more modest. You may skip lunch a few times and donate ten dollars each time to the local food bank. Whatever trials and temptations you face, whatever choices you make, Lent will send you into the wild place of deprivations, sacrifices, and ultimately life-giving transformation. May the Spirit find you in your struggle and sustain you in your wilderness.

Famished Jesus,
in the hollows of your face I see my own hungers
for acceptance, pleasure, power, peace.
I see others' hunger for everything
from bread to prestige to justice.
May the same Spirit who drove you to the desert
drive, sustain, and change me.
May struggling people hear the voice
that proclaimed you beloved
calling them by the same name.
Amen.

Thursday of Week 1

A Desert Riddle

> You shall not oppress a resident alien; you know the heart of an alien, for you were aliens in the land of Egypt.
>
> —Exodus 23:9

Somewhere beneath their seeming amnesia, my people remember ancestral migrations. Stories of forebears driven from their original countries, or exiled in their colonized homelands, are inscribed in the blood. In your body reverberate heartbeats of people who hauled hope and trauma into the future you now call your generation. Look into history. You'll find me there, commanding compassion for strangers akin to your forebears.

Why would anyone choose to go to the desert? It's a deserted place. Desert is another word for godforsaken. But natural deserts cover nearly one-fifth of this God-created earth. Intrinsic to the wholeness, balance, and beauty of creation, deserts diverse in location and kind exist on every continent and are home to one-sixth of the human population.

Some deserts—the Antarctic, for example—are freezing cold. In coastal deserts, such as the Namib of southwestern Africa and the Atacama in northern Chile, weather tends to be mild and even muggy. On all deserts of the world, including those in humid coastal areas, little rain falls. Aridity makes a desert. In places from the southwestern United States to the Gobi region of central Asia, dry conditions give rise to communities of drought-tolerant plants and animals.

I've lived in a dry climate for much of my life. The Sonoran Desert of North America is famous for its iconic, multiarmed Saguaro cactuses. There's one slow-growing Saguaro in front of my Tucson, Arizona, home, beside the sheltering mesquite tree and the red-orange, frilly-bloomed bush called a Mexican Bird of Paradise.

These U.S.-Mexico borderlands, where legions of retirees and "snowbirds" come to get away from the cold, are also notorious for a protracted immigration crisis. In the mid-1990s, to reduce the flow of undocumented migrants from Mexico into the United States, the U.S. Border Patrol enacted a policy of "prevention through deterrence." A government document titled "Border Patrol Strategic Plan: 1994 and Beyond" describes the natural features of the U.S.-Mexico border and the implications for people who might attempt to enter the U.S. illegally: "The border environment is diverse. Mountains, deserts, lakes, rivers and valleys form natural barriers to passage. . . . Illegal entrants crossing through remote, uninhabited expanses of land and sea along the border can find themselves in mortal danger."[1]

The Border Patrol, which began heavily policing urban corridors through which migrants once easily crossed the border, counted on the desert's natural dangers to further deter illegal immigration. Undeterred, however, migrants now walked directly into the desert's mortal dangers. Since the 1990s, thousands of undocumented migrants have died attempting to enter the United States. Migrant advocates, including many Christians, argue that "prevention through deterrence" weaponizes the desert, cruelly causing human suffering and death. Despite undeterred illegal immigration and widespread public criticism of its policies, the Border Patrol kept in place the practices that contributed to the increased migrant death toll. Transborder migration policies of recent U.S. presidential administrations, both Republican and Democrat, have been viewed by many as hardhearted at best.

I remember a meeting I attended in Tucson in the spring of 2000. It was a warm Sunday afternoon. Concerned members of local faith and justice communities crammed into a church social hall containing too few chairs to accommodate everyone. Some people leaned against windowsills while others sat on the floor. Experienced border activists spoke about the need for a grassroots response to the humanitarian crisis happening miles down the road. Despite the dueling egos dynamic that played out when competing pastors took the microphone, a consensus emerged that people of goodwill must collaborate to help their desperate migrant neighbors.

Soon, Humane Borders (*Fronteras Compasivas*) was born. "Motivated by faith and the universal need for kindness," this nonprofit Tucson-based organization "maintains a system of water stations in the Sonoran Desert on routes used by migrants making the perilous journey here on foot." Humane Borders' main mission "is to save desperate people from a horrible death by dehydration and exposure and to create a just and humane environment in the borderlands."[2]

Every undocumented migrant, every Border Patrol officer, every border justice activist, every human being without exception, is cherished by God. Divine love encompasses people otherwise torn apart by their clashing views on immigration. God is as free to work through border guards as through those who view them as the enemy. Partially in response to widespread public criticism of its practices, in 2018, the U.S. Border Patrol established the Missing Migrant Program (MMP) to protect migrants' lives and identify the remains of those who died while traveling on foot. The MMP uses search-and-rescue technology to locate distressed migrants and guide them to assistance. Some say this program offers too little, too late. Others suggest it contributes to God's compassionate work in the world by making the border a bit more humane.

For fortunate desert-dwellers like me, who would never dream of walking long-distance to a land where they wouldn't be welcomed, it's easy to remain oblivious to the dangers the desert poses to unprotected people. One summer afternoon, following a rare and much-needed downpour, I walked with my husband Ken through a wildlife refuge just a few miles north of a border checkpoint. We were there to revel in the water-cooled air of the grassland plain above the desert's elevation. We watched for vermilion flycatchers and gray hawks. I scanned the mesquite branches for birds and the ground for treasures. Ken will tell you I'm a bit ravenlike, always on the lookout for shining things to scavenge. I saw a glint of green near my feet and pulled from the mud what turned out to be a rosary, the kind many migrants carry as they make their way, they pray, to safety. The crucifix pendant was partly broken. Jesus, dying, was missing his right arm. I pocketed the rosary. Later, I rinsed the soil from it and hung it from the rearview mirror of my car.

When I seal myself in this air-conditioned vehicle and drive wherever I want to go, the one-armed crucifix swings from the string of scuffed prayer beads, a tangible reminder of migrants' suffering and their deaths. Sometimes I'm too intent on getting where I'm going to remember the foot traveler who dropped the rosary in the dirt. But at more mindful moments, I do think of the fingers that counted Hail Marys, the heart that contemplated mysteries, the life through which the string of beads once passed, the human being who once passed through this desert or died trying.

I come back to my original question. Why would anyone choose to go to the desert? Reminiscent of that timeworn, pointless riddle in which the chicken crossed the road, an answer comes, more lifeline than punchline: to get to the other side.

God on the move, accompany the travelers.
Whoever they are, whatever their reasons,
watch over the goings and comings
of people in transition.
Let those who enter the desert unready
for merciless terrain and unrelenting heat
get to the other side of desolation
to find shelter, water, and compassion.
Let them find you, Lord, in your mercy.
Let all your beloved people find you.
Lead us to the new life toward which Lent,
this sacred desert season, points.
Amen.

Friday of Week 1

Look at Loss

"Was it not necessary that the Messiah should suffer these things and then enter into his glory?"

(Luke 24:26)

My worshipers, assembled, sing my words, "I will break their hearts of stone."[1] They do not hear themselves as I hear them—fearless, sincere, yet often unaware of my heartbreaking power to reveal the beauty I've concealed inside them. Few dare to know the full meaning of their sacred songs of longing for their crucified and risen Lord. Yet on they sing, lifting up hearts that can only learn to love by being halved like geodes, split open to expose their hidden jewels.

I wrote a spiritual memoir once, and it was published. If I could write it again, I'd write it more truthfully. Not that the book was dishonest. Some readers were surprised by how frank it was. But now I've had more years to reflect on the life stories I recounted and the meanings I made of them. Today I believe I'd come to some truer conclusions.

The more deeply you look, the more, and more clearly, you may see. Lent urges you to look deep into the story of your life so that by the time you get to the end of the season, you can make meaningful connections between your experiences and Jesus' last days before the world lost him forever, or so it seemed.

There is no Lent without loss—indeed, no life without loss. No compassion can come from a heart hardened against the pain of loss. God is merciful and yet allows life to break human hearts. When people feel our wounds and losses, then, in our broken-openness, we can receive compassion—always a gift from God—to help us heal. What we cannot feel cannot be fully healed in us. Through feeling and healing, we become capable of compassion for ourselves and for others suffering loss and pain.

In your Lenten journey through the desert of compassion, you may be tempted to skip over your own losses and wounds. You may have little inclination to write your own memoir or tell your hard stories even to the kindest listener. Is it really necessary to look into yourself before seeking to show others compassion? If you want to make compassion your path, you must first feel your passion, your loves, longings, and losses. These are your teachers, and they tell the truth. They will give you a true feel for yourself. They will help you honor other people's griefs and struggles. Without a clear-eyed gaze into your own wounds and the healing you still may need, your care for others could create the false impression that you're somehow above their messy suffering. Unexamined, unaddressed pain in a person who sets out to help others can lead to abuses of power and the exploitation of vulnerable people.

The losses you've suffered are both personal and communal. You have been betrayed and grieved in life. And you live in a world that in many places has been made a spiritual desert by people who were too rarely shown compassion and so never learned to show it. Brokenness and loss are yours and everyone's, the earth's and Christ's. But this is not the whole truth.

The truth is also this: Resurrection and new life are Christ's and everyone's, the earth's and yours. You'll recognize resurrection when you see it because first you will have looked truly at the losses—your own and the world's—that necessarily precede the risen life. For most people, it's best not to do this alone, but with someone gifted and trained to foster inner healing.

Contemplating your losses will cost you your illusions about events that hurt you and the people involved. The truth you come to see will set you free from fantasies about what happened and its impact. Contemplation of this kind is a spiritual practice that theologian Walter Burghardt calls "a long, loving look at the real."[2] It can lead to your eyes being opened like the eyes of two disciples stumbling through their grief after Jesus' crucifixion (Luke 24:13–35).

They took a long day's desert journey on foot, joined by a stranger who listened with care to their story. They spoke to him as you might speak to a pastoral counselor or spiritual director about a life and a death that changed everything for you. Their listener accepted them while challenging them, too, to see sacred meaning in the losses they described. Near dusk, he sat down to a meal with them, gave thanks, broke bread, and served them. In the breaking and taking, the disciples recognized their fellow traveler as Jesus their Lord, risen from the dead.

Divine compassion—reality regarded with reverence—makes the gravest loss survivable. The risen Christ's compassion made the grieving disciples' hearts catch fire. Once they recognized him, their outlook on all things became illumined by that flame.

Lent calls for a long look into the truth that Holy Week and Easter fully disclose. By *truth,* I don't mean only facts (although evidence and accuracy matter, especially in an era of widespread misinformation). By *truth,* I mean the authentic, honestly perceived; the genuine, lucidly beheld. Such contemplation is sacred work, whether the object beheld is a dull rock split open to reveal sparkling amethysts inside, or the story of Christ's passion, which must be faced before Easter's luminous news can be known.

In the beholder, contemplation cultivates compassion, the capacity to bear witness to what is, without resisting or rejecting it. Look into your life. If you're tempted to look away from the hard parts, don't. Ask someone trustworthy to look alongside you and help you face facts. If you think you've seen it all, revisit the memories anyway. You may be surprised by the insights you'll gain from a deeper gaze. Christians perennially revisit the Jesus story. There's always something more in it to see, some previously unexamined facet newly shining in the firelight.

> *God of revelation and healing,*
> *other people's pain is not my refuge;*
> *my listening is not meant to protect me*
> *from telling my own story of loss.*

Give me eyes to recognize my need to be heard and healed.
Turn me toward someone in whose presence
I can look more deeply and tell more truly
the story of my life, in which I may find you.
Amen.

Saturday of Week 1

Heart of Courage

So I declare and testify together with Christ that you must stop living the kind of life the world lives. Their minds are empty, they have no understanding, they are alienated from the life of God—all because they have hardened their hearts.
—Ephesians 4:17–18, The Inclusive Bible

Unharden your heart. Do what you must. Take the risk of being known, of telling the story of yourself to someone worthy of your trust. Do whatever you can, beloved, to let your heart be loved.

Sometimes my heart goes hard. I can sense it, weighty and solid in my ribcage, pressing dully upward toward my throat. My thoughts turn charcoal grey, the color of apathy, disdain, or worse, contempt. My limbs feel leaden, and I want the day to end, though I have no special evening plans. Maybe sleep, with its dark, restorative medicines, will heal me. Certainly, morning will come, and with it, I hope, a sense of possibility, a softening of the stone in me.

If anything I've just said sounds familiar, maybe you, like me, deal with depression. I regularly work with a skillful, compassionate psychotherapist and take a physician-prescribed antidepressant daily. Most of the time, this combination, along with a healthy diet, exercise, positive relationships, and a meaningful career, means I feel fine and function well. Yet there are days when the emotional burdens accumulate, my heart gets heavy, and it's harder than usual to go normally about my life.

Although I've done it publicly before, it still feels risky to do what I've done here: admit I experience depression and do what I must to manage it. I'm actively resisting the cultural stigma surrounding mental health difficulties. I'm refuting the lie that mood disorders are something shameful to be hidden from view. Yet I acknowledge that for a working pastor to admit in front of God and everybody that she must take steps every day to be mentally OK—well, that's more vulnerability than some folks can stomach. If a pastor isn't immune to depression, who is?

Nobody's immune, although a lot of people work hard not to feel their negative feelings because their family and society taught them emotional pain is impermissible. Sadness is unmanly and anger, unladylike. Fear is cowardice. Grief? That's messy. Get it together.

Working hard not to experience negative emotions can compound the hardship. My own periodic depression stems from the years of emotional hardening I reflexively undertook to make it alive through my early life in a family afflicted by trauma, addiction, and unresolved grief. Children who are told to be quiet and behave nicely when in fact they're suffering and scared have no choice but to do as they're told, lest they be punished or banished from the family on whom their survival depends. The trouble is, silencing feelings and dissociating from painful realities can petrify your heart and turn your inner world into an emotional desert.

"Without emotion," writes psychiatry professor Victoria Beckner, "the landscape of our choices looks like a flat grey desert without any landmarks indicating what is important."[1] It's to such internally flattened, spiritually colorless people that Paul refers in his Letter to the Ephesians: "Their minds are empty, they have no understanding, they are alienated from the life of God—all because they have hardened their hearts" (4:18 TIB). Paul urges the Ephesians to re-associate with themselves, their feelings, and God.

Reconnecting with hardened, hidden feelings within you can be difficult and scary work that requires support and persistence. "We have to develop the muscle and courage to stay with this uncomfortable welter of emotions in order to unpack what is important and meaningful," says Beckner.[2] Rooted in the Latin word *cor*, meaning "heart," courage is the lifeblood of a person who's afraid yet willing to feel the emotions beneath the fear. Petrified feelings, once unearthed and experienced, tell a true story of your life. Emotions signify what matters most to you and help you make choices according to your deepest values.

The prospect of living with awareness and integrity, in touch with the God who gave you the capacity to feel, makes venturing into the interior, emotional desert worth the effort. When Jesus struggled with temptation in the arid Judean wilderness, his deeply felt fidelity to the vision and values that mattered most to him empowered him to resist the tempter's wiles and stay connected with God. Once he'd withstood his desert trial, Jesus had developed courage enough to emerge from solitude and begin his ministry of compassion. Nothing was more important or meaningful to Jesus than embodying God's compassion. The people who experienced his healing, instruction, and companionship in turn embodied compassion toward themselves and others.

This is how compassion works. It permeates your porous heart, you offer it forward, you receive more from the sacred source of it, and then you have more to give. Whether you offer acts of caregiving, teaching, befriending, or helping, your compassion will only be sustainable if you return, again and always, to its holy source, who is God. Prayer is God-centered self-compassion. Worship at its best feels good because it not only glorifies God; it also replenishes the hearts of people who know they need compassion and spiritual sustenance.

You'll not find a better model of self-compassion than Jesus. The Gospels testify to his self-compassionate practices of solitary prayer, close friendship, meal-sharing, even his sleeping when under stress and weeping when grieved. All these exemplify a person who honored his feelings and treated himself with the same loving-kindness he offered to others. Jesus didn't serve from an empty cup, and neither can you. I certainly can't. To live this life wholly, stay connected with God, and sustain a vocation of compassion, I need soul-replenishing gifts. These include my marriage to the love of my life, walks in the desert, dinners with friends, phone conversations with my BFF, caring colleagues, psychotherapy, chocolate, the companionship of cats, and a contemplative writing practice, among other good things. What do you need? How will you express sacred self-compassion as you press deeper into the Lenten desert?

Give me courage,
God of my heart,
to let myself feel the reality of this day,
whatever it may bring.
I want to live fully,
not numbed, but awake
to the gift of my being
in you.
Amen.

Week 2

Reach Out Your Hand

Sabbath Rest Stop

A natural disaster, unnaturally intensified by climate change, has gouged a wide swath of destruction and death through communities that will never again be what they were. Antidemocratic movement is posing such a threat to this society's electoral process that some commentators call it "a democratic emergency" and "a five-alarm fire." A friend who went off her antidepressants has said she can't manage without them and needs to talk to her doctor. Results of another friend's medical scans reveal the need for a biopsy. Ringing in my ears is the conversation I had yesterday with a shocked and grieving man whose unvaccinated loved one recently died of COVID-19. You get the idea. You live in the same world in which I live, where things are tough all over.

In last week's reflections, I poked holes in the notion that toughening up is a desirable response to life's hardships. I urged you to unharden your heart and develop emotional fluency in your Lenten quest for deepened compassion. I acknowledged how scary and difficult it can be to feel and regulate the full range of emotions that your Creator designed you to experience. I urged you not to go it alone.

This week, I'm doubling down on that last part: don't go it alone. Reach out your hand. Even if the global pandemic has put you off handshakes as a gesture of greeting, reach out your hand in ways that are sensible and safe for you and others. Encounter, really encounter, another human being who is as vulnerable as you are, or more so. Reach out your heart. Openhearted connection with another child of God makes compassion real—not just a virtue, but a practice, a way of living well with others.

It's Sunday. Can you go to church this morning, or have you already attended worship today? I hope you have access to a faith community where you can connect meaningfully with God and God's people.

At the church I serve, we no longer shake hands or hug when we pass the peace of Christ during worship. Our restraint is meant to reduce the spread of infection among the gathered people who comprise the body of Christ. I miss the easy, appropriate touches that once were an unquestioned aspect of Sunday worship, but I don't let nostalgic sentiment override good sense. I encourage each of us, when passing the (now contactless) peace of Christ, to press our own hands together prayerfully at heart-level and bow slightly toward each other. It's akin to an ancient, ritual gesture of reverent respect that I first experienced when praying with Benedictine monks, who greet and treat each other and all their guests as Christ. I love the way it works liturgically. People honor and protect one another. They keep their hands to themselves, but mutually, they reach out their hearts. Surely God is blessed between them.

"In the parched deserts of postmodernity," wrote John O'Donohue, "a blessing can be like the discovery of a fresh well. It would be lovely if we could rediscover our power to bless one another."[1] News of disaster, depression, disease, and death feels to me like a dispatch from the parched deserts of postmodernity. But as suffering is endemic to every era, so the fresh well of blessing that flows from God's heart is eternal yet current. Compassion is the substance of the blessings people can bestow on one another. May the readings for each day of the week ahead bless the hand you extend to give and receive God's compassion.

Monday of Week 2

Thomas, Transformed

But Thomas (who was called the Twin), one of the twelve, was not with them when Jesus came. So the other disciples told him, "We have seen the Lord." But he said to them, "Unless I see the mark of the nails in his hands, and put my finger in the mark of the nails and my hand in his side, I will not believe."
—John 20:24–25

Scandalous, aren't they, the lengths to which I'll go to receive the startled touch of an incredulous soul? I cherish the faithful, as the faithful well know. But it's the unbeliever, the holdout, for whose transformation I take the most extreme measures of love.

Some interpreters of Thomas's story set out to redeem him. They critique timeworn, negative portrayals of "doubting Thomas" and affirm his intelligent need for a tactile encounter with his Lord. They question the wisdom of a faith that doesn't ask questions.

Here are my questions. Where was Thomas when Jesus appeared, having been raised from the dead? Before Jesus died, how was Thomas's relationship with the other disciples, who on Easter trembled fearfully in that locked room where the miraculous later happened? Did Thomas share a close and trusting relationship with the other disciples? Or was his skepticism about their Easter experience typical of his attitude toward them all along?

I find it hard to muster compassion for Thomas—not because he prefers the scientific method over unseeing credulity; that kind of toughmindedness I can appreciate. But Thomas made an idol of empirical research. Proof was the only means by which his dubious mind could be changed. His demand for hands-on evidence mattered more to him than the changed disciples whose testimony he dismissed. I'm troubled by Thomas's knee-jerk refutation of their impassioned witness to the most significant event of their lives. They encountered Jesus risen from the dead. How hardheaded must a person be to deny others' lived experience? Thomas would have been right at home among those who disbelieved the women who'd discovered Jesus' tomb to be empty. The women's Easter proclamation, according to those cynics, was nothing more than "an idle tale."

"Cynics may dismiss compassion as touchy-feely or irrational," writes an unnamed author at *Greater Good Magazine*.[1] Ironically, Thomas became literally touchy-feely when Jesus, risen, fulfilled his demand for tangible evidence:

> A week later his disciples were again in the house, and Thomas was with them. Although the doors were shut, Jesus came and stood among them and said, "Peace be with you." Then he said to Thomas, "Put your finger here and see my hands. Reach out your hand and put it in my side. Do not doubt but believe." Thomas answered him, "My Lord and my God!" Jesus said to him, "Have you believed because you have seen me? Blessed are those who have not seen and yet have come to believe." (John 20:26–29)

The story about Thomas is more than an account of an unbeliever in resurrection whose doubts were dispelled by verifiable proof. By urging Thomas to reach out and feel the open wounds of crucifixion in his living body, Jesus invited him to awaken. The God who overcomes evil and death is active whenever people truly see and bravely touch the hurting human beings before them. After Thomas lived alone for a week in the desert of his Easter disbelief, Jesus returned to resurrect Thomas's dead-and-buried compassion.

Could it be that Jesus' wounds were healed by Thomas's astonished, tender touch? It could be. A compassionate reading of the Gospel allows for transformative possibilities beyond the written text. The Gospels exist not just to convince you of their veracity, but to call you beyond your limited beliefs, to open your mind, heart, and hands to God's free, redeeming movement throughout creation.

Thomas reached beyond himself and the limits he'd set around his life. Jesus speaks to you and me the same words—*reach out your hand*—that he spoke to Thomas. If you're at all like Thomas (and if I'm honest, I am), the desert you inhabit may be a condition of spiritual seclusion. You may be protecting yourself from contact with people as stubborn as Thomas, or as wild, wounded, and implausible as Jesus with his exposed, grave-raw flesh.

Peace be with you, he says again and again to his frightened, grieving followers. Jesus insists on breathing out peace despite the grisly violence of his public execution. It's unbelievable, as Thomas could tell you, until it isn't.

Unkillable life takes hold of your hand and makes you capable of a faith so vulnerable you fear you might die of it. You don't. You stay there, hand outstretched toward someone broken and hurting, receiving from you compassion you didn't know you had in you. All that's left for you to do is pray with Thomas, transformed: *My Lord and my God.*

My Lord, my God,
you're not mine alone
but everyone's. Create in me
the capacity to touch another life
with empathy and kindness
that reveal your risen presence.
Amen.

Tuesday of Week 2

Rain of God

I stretch out my hands to you;
my soul thirsts for you like a parched land.
—Psalm 143:6

When you reach out to me, I reach back to you. I pour myself
out like water. Drink, beloved, and let your soul be replen-
ished by my mercy, which never runs dry.

In the brilliant triple-digit days of a Sonoran June, the empty sky burns hard, a vast blue tile in a firing kiln. Road signs that read, "Do not enter when flooded," look laughable—as though this scorched earth could ever be flooded.

Eventually, clouds roll in overhead. It takes days for them to accumulate. Luminous and pillowy, they offer the gracious gift of shade and the promise of water. Desert dwellers practically fall to our knees in obeisance. At last, temperatures drop and the clouds break open, sending storms plummeting to the dry earth.

Unlike the lush, oozy rains of wetter climates where storm sewer systems run underground, Sonoran Desert monsoons come on fast and flashy, full of windy water and shocking power. Roadways usually bone-dry suddenly flood, much to the disbelief of some drivers, whose failed, expensive attempts to drive vehicles on flooded roads prompted the creation in 1995 of Arizona's so-called "stupid motorist law." Arizona Revised Statute 28-910 makes scofflaw motorists "liable for the expenses of any emergency response." In other words, those *Do not enter when flooded* signs mean business. They mean you'll pay for your own rescue, at least in theory. In practice, the law is rarely enforced because authorities don't want flood-endangered people to avoid calling for help. What first responders really want is for people to heed the National Weather Service's pithy warning: *Turn around don't drown.*

"Turn around don't drown" sounds almost religious, akin to "Repent and be saved." Prompted by negative consequences including regret, repentance amounts to a change of mind and behavior. Most drivers rescued from drowning in a storm-flooded desert arroyo surely regret having taken that risk. The trauma must cause them to repent of driving into deep, moving water.

Why did they ignore those bright yellow flood-warning signs in the first place? When asked this question, University of Arizona Psychiatry Professor Ole Thienhause offered a humbling answer: "The human capacity to evaluate risk is a very questionable proposition."[1] So, is it really a "stupid motorist" who bypasses barricades in a monsoon? Or is it a person no stupider than you or me, no less deserving of compassion, who humanly underestimates the trouble ahead?

"Of all of Arizona's odd laws, the one that applies to penalizing idiot drivers for getting stuck in washes and flooded underpasses is my favorite. If you somehow think it's okay to drive through a water-covered area where water wouldn't normally be, you deserve to get punished,"[2] wrote a Tucson-based contributor to a free weekly newspaper. The same journalist had been fired from a daily newspaper for posting remarks on social media that appeared to make light of, and even encourage, local homicides.

It seems this journalist possessed a questionable capacity to evaluate the professional risk of expressing public sarcasm on the topic of murder. Was he stupider than the average person? I doubt it. But his words were unkinder than you or I may hope to be. His punitive views on violators of Arizona's "turn around don't drown" law suggest an embittered lack of compassion that's become common in public discourse. Therefore—and here's where the difficult Christian imperative of unconditional neighbor-love comes in—he was probably in need of an outstretched hand from someone who could see him for the vulnerable person he was behind his merciless rhetoric.

Just because such a one won't accept your outstretched hand, doesn't mean you don't offer it

"But I say to you," says Jesus to us all, "Love your enemies and pray for those who persecute you, so that you may be children of your Father in heaven; for he makes his sun rise on the evil and on the good, and sends rain on the righteous and on the unrighteous" (Matt. 5:44–45). These are the words of a wise and merciful desert dweller. Jesus' God-talk reflects his deep faith and his feel for the desert's heat, light, and much-needed rains, which fall on the just and the unjust alike. Jesus' commandments include no punitive laws that shame rescued people for the reckless, regrettable decisions that landed them in trouble. No one's exempt from Jesus' compassion, nor from his summons to love even hard-to-love enemies whose hearts seem as parched as a desert in a drought.

God of heaven and earth,
may this season of Lent turn me around
before I run headlong into danger and regret.
May your loving-kindness soak into me
and change me into someone who treats other people
as graciously as you treat me.
Amen.

Wednesday of Week 2

Why and Yet

Why do you hold back your hand; why do you keep your
hand in your bosom?
Yet God my King is from of old, working salvation in the
earth.

—Psalm 74:11–12

*My hand holds the heavens into which you shout your ques-
tions. I hear you even as I hear every birdsong, every mur-
mur of human-made devices meant to move their users closer
to the answers they seek. How dear to me are all my creatures, from the computational problem solvers to the winged
beings calling for their mates. And how dear to me are you.*

Driving home in winter dusk, listening to the radio, I heard a news
announcer speak the words that once were beyond my imagining: "no
end in sight to the pandemic."

Why is God allowing it? A day or two before I heard the radio
announcer's bleak forecast, I'd asked this of my husband Ken, who
knows better than to proffer easy theological answers. My question
resembled those the psalmist asked of God: *Why do you hold back your
hand? Why do you keep your hand in your bosom?* Such demands for
divine explanation pertain to any age. Why does God, who is good,
permit evil and suffering? Philosophers call this the question of the-
odicy, which literally means *justifying God*.

It wasn't a pandemic that prompted the psalmist's desperate yet prayerful plea for an answer, but the Jerusalem temple's destruction by violent enemies of Israel. Faced with this appalling desecration, the psalmist "justified" God by not presuming to do so. The Holy One of Israel needs no human advocate. No reasoned argument can do justice to the One of whom the psalmist humbly cries, despite all countervailing evidence, *Yet God my King is from of old, working salvation in the earth.*

Yet God. This is the fierce faith-confession of a human whose questions to the King go unanswered. That mortals can't conceive of the Salvation Worker's holy ways seems only to intensify the psalmist's conviction that God is universally good. God's inexplicably permissive hand allows enemies to persecute God's people and demolish the divine dwelling place while that same hand reaches *in the earth,* beneath the surface of creation. God plants seeds of salvation deeper down than even the temple's foundations.

Why God allows the temple's destruction, the global pandemic, the crises that sweep away so much from so many, I would be a fool to try to say. I can hope, however, to be like the psalmist, holy fool enough to believe God is good all the time.

When God's hand remains tucked away behind a cloak of clouds while the planet reels from the catastrophic impact of human hubris, I want to trust enough in the goodness of that hidden, holy hand to extend my own in compassion to somebody who needs to know we're not alone in this life. Could my own hand point toward an answer to the psalmist's agonized *why?* Could it be that God, in baffling hands-off benevolence, refrains from handling problems we're meant to face together, hand in hand? My hands are free to do the work that's mine, which today is to write for you this Lenten reminder: You're not alone in the desert you traverse.

Perhaps you know already, but if you don't, you will be made to know whose life you're called to bless by your hand outstretched in friendship, service, artmaking, prayer—some expression of practical compassion. First, let your hands simply rest, upturned, receptive. Take the time you're given now to breathe and pray, breathe and pray, expecting no answer to your heart's plaintive *why*, expecting only to be shown the next compassionate thing to do and with whom.

If you're led into the company of those who foresee no end of struggle, you might be tempted to answer their *whys* with platitudes like *everything happens for a reason* or *God will never give you more than you can handle*. Resist these patent falsehoods. Oversimplifying mysteries of evil and pain can only prove unwise and, sometimes, unkind. Human unknowing is uneasy by divine design. Let it be so. Unknowing drives all human wondering and ultimately lands you where you're meant to be, not in a state of comfortable certainty but in honest solidarity with other searching people. Though many of our questions go unanswered, together we can cross the desert stretches of this earth in which our God, Sovereign from of old, is working our salvation even now.

Reach out your hand, O God,
to the beings reaching out to you
for help and answers. Reach out
your hand through the hands
of helpers wise enough to understand
what they can and cannot do.
Reach me, I pray, and find me ready
to do the work that's mine,
to put the time and gifts you've given me
to needed use.
Amen.

Thursday of Week 2

Burnout and Oases in the Desert

> Then suddenly a woman who had been suffering from hemorrhages for twelve years came up behind him and touched the fringe of his cloak, for she said to herself, "If I only touch his cloak, I will be made well." Jesus turned, and seeing her he said, "Take heart, daughter; your faith has made you well." And instantly the woman was made well.
>
> —Matthew 9:20–22

The patterns you see in the dust are fringe-swept signs that I walk before you, just a footfall ahead. If you will only take heart and take hold of my cloak, I will lead you back to the source of your life.

Some of the people I minister to are overextended, overworked, under-resourced, verging on burnout or already there. Unrealistic expectations of work can exacerbate burnout. Journalist Derek Thompson writes about how "workism," a faulty, labor-centered "religion" is a cause of the problem:

> Some people worship beauty, some worship political identities, and others worship their children. But everybody worships something. And workism is among the most potent of the new religions competing for congregants. . . . A culture that funnels its dreams of self-actualization into salaried jobs is setting itself up for collective anxiety, mass disappointment and inevitable burnout.[1]

Many people have replaced faith in God and commitment to a spiritual community with work, seeking not only to earn a livelihood but also to forge a reason for being, a system of values, a life of meaning. Toiling for money, esteem, or even an honorable cause cannot heal people or keep them spiritually whole. Work is not the Creator, Redeemer, or Sustainer of life.

When all your efforts and hours have left you depleted, searching for an oasis—a patch of shade, a spring of fresh water, a place of rest, a compassionate helper—you've wound up in the spiritual desert that is burnout, exhaustion at every level of your being. Your body is deeply fatigued. Your emotional resources are spent. Your mental agility is thwarted. You're like the woman in the Gospel story who suffered hemorrhages for twelve years. Unrelenting stress in your work and personal life have left you with barely the strength to crawl and grope for the fringe of a potential healer's cloak.

The word *burnout* connotes the desert's most fearsome features. As scarce water, scorching heat, and scant vegetation make for uninhabitable land that threatens the lives of those who venture there unprepared, so do excessive labor, low wages, and a dehumanizing workplace make for burnout. But not only low-wage workers burn out. High-income earners and unpaid volunteers in congregations and service agencies are also susceptible. Burnout can happen to all kinds of workers, but it always results from demand exceeding supply. The demand, sometimes self-imposed, for energy, effort, hours, and stamina exceeds available supplies of money, rest, perquisites, emotional support, and the spiritual wherewithal that sustain people and equip them to thrive in their work.

Sometimes burnout takes the form of compassion fatigue, common among health care workers and people laboring in ministry and human service fields. Traumatized, struggling patients', clients', or congregants' needs for compassion continually exceed providers' external and inner resources. Exhausted care providers suffer harm in dysfunctional systems meant to offer healing.

People in communities historically expected to nurture others at their own expense, particularly women of color, stand a greater-than-average risk of burnout. People like me, who have unearned, undeserved racial and social privilege are morally obligated to help dismantle systems that exploit the labor and shorten the lives of those pushed to society's margins. Compassion consists in part of striving for social equity. Compassion requires privileged people to make sacrifices so their overworked neighbors can finally find rest.

Crucial for anyone who practices compassion is to take a weekly sabbath and periodic, longer sabbaticals for physical recovery, spiritual renewal, and emotional restoration. A commitment to regular time off and rest is necessary for any compassion practice to be sustainable and lead to constructive transformation rather than a crash-and-burn demise.

Sabbaths and sabbaticals are biblical, God-commanded, re-creative visits to oases of replenishment in the desert. Yours need not be costly or luxurious. You might make it your regular discipline to disconnect from your phone and read a book one day each week. You might take a staycation and resist the temptation to check your email or answer any work-related call. Whatever you do, take regular breaks, frequent breathers. Before you get thirsty, take a long cool drink at the oasis in your desert, whether that consists of contemplative prayer or a conversation with a friend who loves you no matter what. Protect your compassionate heart from being charred by the searing difficulties you may witness among the people you serve.

Take a long, loving look at your calendar and obligations. Plan, soon if you can, to dedicate a day to rest. Schedule a future sabbatical. Make rest a part of your Lenten observance and your everyday life. Do what you must to prevent the hemorrhaging of your strength and the burning out of your light. Like the woman who summoned the humble courage to touch Jesus' cloak and be made well, reach out your own trembling hand to a trustworthy helper who can put you in touch with God's restorative mercies.

God of loving-kindness, you know my fatigue,
my hemorrhages, and capacities.
I am reaching out to you to be made well.
Heal me and help me understand
that only from the well of my own well-being
can I extend compassion to another soul.
Amen.

Friday of Week 2

Move with Compassion

As they were leaving Jericho, a large crowd followed him. There were two blind men sitting by the roadside. When they heard that Jesus was passing by, they shouted, "Lord, have mercy on us, Son of David!" The crowd sternly ordered them to be quiet; but they shouted even more loudly, "Have mercy on us, Lord, Son of David!" Jesus stood still and called them, saying, "What do you want me to do for you?" They said to him, "Lord, let our eyes be opened." Moved with compassion, Jesus touched their eyes. Immediately they regained their sight and followed him.

—Matthew 20:29–34

Here is my mercy, here is my hand. I lay it over your eyes. It never was you who could not see. But now, I have heard you; now you are free. Come, my beloved. Come, follow me.

Here, near the end of Lent's second week, you've been reflecting with me for several days on the invitation to reach out your hand, to receive and give compassion. Today we read a biblical story of compassion requested, offered, and accepted. It's a story of cruelty and of holy kindness that overcomes it.

Two men who are blind have been pushed to the social margins (a desert roadside) and silenced by those who don't want to hear the voices of people with disabilities. Jesus hears the men's outcries for mercy. He welcomes them to come to the center of God's attention, to receive the respect and care that their neighbors deny them. Not only is the men's eyesight restored, but their inmost selves are also transformed. They become capable of seeing who Jesus is: mercy embodied, the One who will lead them to live a life of visionary love for God, themselves, and others. The healed men follow Jesus; they move with the compassion that has saved them.

To move with compassion is to dance with the Spirit, freed from the meanness of the crowd that shouts down the voices of the vulnerable and casts them out of public view. When Jesus opens the eyes of people with disabilities, he affirms their visibility as well as their capacity to recognize God's truth and move according to it. They were whole people before Jesus' mercy changed their bodies and abilities. Now they *know* their God-given wholeness, dignity, and worth. Never again will they sit on the sidelines, disempowered by people whose self-importance drives them to dominate and silence others.

The healed men refrain from retaliating against the people who treated them like roadside trash. The insight they gain from Jesus' compassionate touch evidently includes awareness that following him means resisting the impulse to inflict cruelty even on the perpetrators of it.

Following Jesus means moving with compassion, synchronizing your steps with those of the peacemaking Lord whose love disrupts cycles and systems of oppression and violence. Whenever Jesus confronted religious authorities, he challenged their values and behaviors without attacking their humanity.

Compassion coursed through Jesus, sometimes urgently, often tenderly, as when he listened to the pair of men who were blind. In their shouts for mercy, it seems he heard the voice of all hurting humankind and it stopped him in his tracks. For the moment that "Jesus stood still," before he could be moved or move with compassion, he was, I surmise, immobilized by the pain he empathically felt.

People of compassion allow others' suffering to pierce their defenses. When your neighbors' cries enter your ears, the pain becomes no longer theirs alone. Such a vulnerable encounter warrants a pause, a moment of stillness, a silent listening to God, who is present in the plea for mercy and in the mercy, itself, which you may offer. Others' pain and needs also warrant a gut check on your part. Responding with compassion to others who are suffering does not mean acting in a boundaryless way. Your safety, capacities, and limitations are crucial to respect.

Take time today to stand still in your interior desert, by the Jericho road that runs through your imagination. Quiet yourself and listen. A voice may come into your awareness, both begging for mercy and offering it. The outcry you hear may arise from your own throat. In the silence or the noise of your still moment, claim this assurance: God is present to you at the intersection of crying need and lovingkindness. You can embody both.

If you are afraid, see your fear for what it may be: the survival instinct of a threatened or discarded child of God. Without lashing out at others, do what you must to keep this child safe. Protect the one who's been cast off like so much roadside trash. Place your outstretched hand over your beloved heart. Its thrumming is God's compassion coursing ceaselessly through you, less a virtue than a lifeforce. Move to its beat and follow its summons.

God in my blood, in my hands and heart,
God in my life and losses, my eyes and cries,
have mercy on me, on all the criers, on all the silenced ones.
Have mercy—because you are mercy—
even on those who fail to recognize you
at the roadside, you at the margins,
you whose compassion calls
the marginalized to the center
and moves those once immobilized
to follow you.
Amen.

Saturday of Week 2

Hold Your Own

The Lord is my chosen portion and my cup; you hold my lot. The boundary lines have fallen for me in pleasant places; I have a goodly heritage.

—Psalm 16:5–6

Blessed are you when you shield yourself and others from abuse. Blessed are you when you refuse to be reviled and when you protect yourself from persecution. I do not call you or anyone to be maligned or mistreated. Blessed are you when you uphold your dignity as my beloved one and resist the urge to return evil for the evil done to you.

Sometimes, with your outstretched hand, you must set and hold a boundary. To keep yourself safe and protect others from abuse, your extended hand must uphold a barrier to prevent misconduct and injury. Behavioral boundary-keeping is an act of compassion for yourself and for anyone at risk of being mistreated.

For followers of Jesus, who teaches his disciples to love our enemies, boundary-setting can be extremely challenging. The church has largely failed to teach Christians how to love our enemies while resisting their abuse. Moreover, throughout history, women have been societally conditioned to nurture others, acquiesce to aggressors, and efface ourselves. Therefore, many women find it impossible to resist violators' transgressions.

Instead of flashing the palm of the hand to say *stop*, those who have never been taught to protect themselves commonly reach for their abuser's hand. Placating gestures of outreach, rooted in victims' trauma and fear of further abuse, can foster an abuser's imagined righteousness and convey seeming permission to continue the abuse. Whether physical, sexual, emotional, or spiritual, abuse of any kind is wrong, unacceptable, and inexcusable.

Abusers must be stopped. Bullies and aggressors must be prevented from further hurting others. They must be held accountable for the suffering they have caused. They must not be enabled to persist in inflicting on others the pain and brokenness in their own bodies and souls.

Abusers were abused. They were victims, themselves. That's how they learned to lash out and victimize others. Abusers reproduce the wounds they were made to suffer.

God's compassion for humankind extends to the most vicious, damaging people in the form of tough love. You and I can understand these things and affirm divine capacities far beyond our own. But spiritual humility and insight into the origins of abuse neither protect victims nor exempt abusers from respecting boundaries that shield others from emotional or physical violence.

An abuser's contrite awareness of culpability is the necessary precondition to receiving forgiveness. Through a truly humble, sorrowful admission of guilt, an abuser can become capable of accepting forgiveness and loving-kindness. After taking responsibility, showing remorse, and making amends for the damage inflicted, an abuser may be invited to participate in a mutually compassionate relationship—preferably with someone who has not been previously victimized by the abuser. The wounds at the heart of the abuser's misconduct may be healed by transformative experiences with people who have learned to hold their own boundaries, but this is a rare outcome, difficult to achieve.

Compassion is not cheap. It's costly. It's not nice. It's fierce. Compassion in the context of abuse entails taking a stand with people who have been degraded, victimized, and silenced. In solidarity with those who have been made to suffer, compassion consists of resistance to behaviors and systems that dehumanize anyone. This is not to say abusers should be dehumanized; contempt and retaliation only perpetuate cyclical abuse. For abusers to stand a chance of undergoing reformation, they must receive the respect they fail to show others. Their inherent human dignity must be affirmed by people with strong boundaries who are trained and skilled at keeping themselves and others safe.

I say all this to you as a person who has learned through hard, repeated experience to resist emotional abuse. Like many clergy-women, I have been targeted by emotionally dysregulated people. With alarming frequency, emotionally wounded churchgoers treat clergy in leadership roles, especially women, as surrogate objects of their unprocessed rage. I have been yelled at, insulted, belittled, threatened, loudly disrupted while leading worship, and blamed for pain I did not cause. Jeanne Stevenson-Moessner invokes G. Lloyd Rediger's analysis of the person who abuses clergy: "His or her actions are spurred by factors such as childhood trauma, projections, transferences, violent role models, inadequate socialization, personality disorders, or authoritarian issues."[1]

Once, when I refused to accept emotional abuse (shaming, name calling, and sarcasm), an angry churchgoer sneered, "You and your boundaries." Yes. My boundaries and me. They're good for me and exemplary for others. Drs. Henry Cloud and John Townsend have famously written, "Maintaining your boundaries is good for other people; it will help them learn what their families of origin did not teach them: to respect other people."[2]

Your exemplary boundaries may be the closest thing to compassion that you can show to some people. Hold your boundaries for your own sake, regardless of what others may learn or (more likely) how they may resent you for refusing to be degraded, manipulated, or controlled. People who have never learned to respect others are highly unlikely to appreciate "you and your boundaries." Never has a person who tried to hurt or humiliate me later thanked me for the lesson in respect.

Don't do it for kudos. Develop and maintain your boundaries because you are a beloved person of God, inherently worthy of respect, dignity, and care. Cultivate your self-awareness and seek healing for any abuse you have suffered. Hold firm boundaries and abusers will desert you, frustrated by your refusal to cower. There you'll be then, blooming in the desert of holy self-compassion, where healthy relationships with others can flourish. You'll experience the meaning of the psalmist's words: "The boundary lines have fallen for me in pleasant places" (16:6).

Thank you, God, my protector and refuge,
for shielding me and showing me my worth.
You have called me by name, called me your own,
and called me to respect myself and others.
To those who have been violated,
send help and healing.
Embolden family and community members
to keep each other safe.
Let your Spirit govern the human conscience
so that abusers are stopped and held accountable
and your people learn not to harm
but to honor one another.
Amen.

Week 3

Stay Awake with Me

Sabbath Rest Stop

We were 22 and 25, newlyweds embarking on our honeymoon in Mexico. My husband Ken's aunt, Cheryl, co-owned a time-share condominium near Manzanillo. Her wedding gift to us was a two-week stay. All we had to do was rent a VW Beetle at the airport in Puerto Vallarta and make the four-hour drive through, as it turned out, deeper darkness than two city kids accustomed to constant artificial light had ever witnessed. The road had no shoulder. Trees thickly, blackly bordered its edges. On one stretch of the journey, the car's weak headlights dimly illumined armies of tarantulas crawling across the pavement like a living carpet. At another point, a man darted into the road, frantically waving his arms. We, who possessed no mobile phone, no first aid kit, and no Spanish to speak of, drove on, feeling stricken, never to know if we'd failed to help someone in need or avoided falling victim to roadside bandits.

I sat, startled and alert in the passenger seat. Several kilometers later, we passed through a village where lamps were burning in some windows. I saw a hand-lettered sign and grabbed my Spanish-English traveler's dictionary. *Abierto* meant "open." We pulled over to buy a few provisions—Cokes in glass bottles, Bimbo brand toasted bread, and fresh eggs with bits of hay stuck to their shells. Once we'd resumed heading south through the soft night air, Ken asked me to stay awake and keep him company as he drove us deeper into this unfamiliar land. But after a while, I could no longer keep my eyes *abierto*. It turned out I was coming down with strep throat, though we wouldn't know it for another forty-eight hours.

Maybe for you, entering Lent's third week feels a little like the trip

I've just described. Maybe there's both a sense of venturing beyond the borders of the known world and a lulling quality about the season's slow, even ominous, self-revelation. You're well past Lent's introductory days. You're in the desert now, approaching its center. The honeymoon, if there was one, is over. And what will you discover? Why do you press on?

Days, the wheels of your life, roll on. You move forward, onward, and yet Lent's destination is as far ahead of you as its beginning is behind you. Stay the course. Stay awake, present to the unspectacular present. Proceed wakefully. Make the effort, especially when boredom or unease cause you to wonder why you're bothering. Go ahead and wonder: How can a season of scarcity and sacrifice invented by the church, an institution some say is archaic, lead you to any place worth going in such a world as this, where suffering is endless but so are the entertainments that can distract you from it all?

Wonder, but resist your heart's temptation to harden. If you notice your hands, those extensions of the heart, frequently wringing or clenching into fists, give them a rest, a compassionate respite from the work of compassion for others. Respect your fatigue and your limits, lest distress tear you to pieces. Literally, *distress* means *stretch apart*. People beside themselves, torn asunder from within, need to be restored to wholeness, as I needed penicillin when I had strep throat. By the way, the medicine worked. It enabled my body to heal and saved our honeymoon.

If you're wounded, you're called to be healed; when you're healed, you're called to compassion for the wounded. These callings necessarily intersect and intertwine. Your woundedness is a source of your compassion. "The great illusion . . . is to think that [humankind] can be led out of the desert by someone who has never been there."[1] Not only have you been there; you are invited in this middle week of Lent to reflect on distress and the desert as a metaphor for it. The desert can be any situation in which destructive powers threaten to separate creature from Creator, to separate you from the One who gives you life. Yet the desert, too, can be a place of holy stillness where creature and Creator are rejoined, where you remember that God remembers you.

God remembers you every hour, every day. It's Sunday. If possible, devote an hour of this day to worshiping with others. Be reminded that whatever may distress you these days, a greater, unifying love than all destructive forces holds you close. God holds everyone close. Starting tomorrow, you and I will consider distress, and we'll keep at it for a week. But be of good courage. Distress tolerance is a God-given human capacity. It can be cultivated and put to compassionate use.

Monday of Week 3

Where the Aloes Grow

It was I who fed you in the wilderness, in the land of drought.
—Hosea 13:5

Downpours may be rare where you find yourself, but I infuse the air you breathe, the Spirit you receive, with moisture. I made you of flesh and bone and fluid; you contain a sea you cannot see.

In the desert, aloes, shrubby succulents, flourish. They grow in green rosettes, their long, meaty leaves rich with internal gel. Aloe contains protective properties and healing medicines, especially good for burnt, dry, or abraded skin. The resilience of the aloes in our yard amazes me. We relocated several from one location to another, but we weren't quick about it. For a while they lay around in uprooted heaps, turning grey. Once we transplanted them, we gave them scant attention. But they prosper anyway, full of chlorophyll, sending up tall, blooming stems. Hummingbirds buzz about their nectar-seeking business, nosing into the aloes' coral-colored, tubular flowers.

Like other succulents and cacti, aloes tolerate drought. Their capacity to adapt to dry conditions, store up moisture in their flesh, enrich the air, and feed the birds makes them a juicy metaphor for people who tolerate distress and treat distressed people with compassion.

Distress is an umbrella term for negative emotions such as sadness, anger, anxiety, frustration, and fear. Think of distress as your felt response to life when its sweet waters run low. The sun by day burns holes in your shelter. The chill of night creeps in through the walls. Your supplies of patience, hope, and humor get all but depleted, and the challenges keep coming, the bills keep coming due.

Distress tolerance consists of your emotional surplus, your ability in tough times to draw deeply on stores of inner strength and coping capacities, as an aloe rooted in dry soil thrives greenly on its stockpiled, internal water. Your distress tolerance differs from that of others. Maybe you're unflappable under pressure (and emotionally cautious even on joyful occasions). Or maybe "passionate" is a polite word for how riled you can get when stressed (but your passion also means you celebrate the good times with gusto).

Like much in emotional life, your distress tolerance is derived in part from your early, formative experiences and examples. If, when distressed, your primary childhood caregivers spun themselves into a tempest or drank away the pain, chances are you didn't develop desert succulent abilities to take intense emotional heat. This is not to say you're defective if emotional distress is hard for you to tolerate. You get to be who you are, how you are, without shouldering the added burden of pathologizing judgment. Sure, it helps to have been raised by grown-ups who didn't go to pieces when circumstances stretched them, but if that's not your history, OK, it's not your history. You still get to live in the present with loving self-regard and look to the future with confidence that God is already there, doing good.

You may be someone who needs to take extra care to cultivate distress tolerance. If you find unpleasant emotions such as sadness, anger, and fear tough to bear, try making it a practice to notice your feelings, identifying where and how in your body they show up. Sit mindfully with the sensations in an attitude of acceptance rather than reactivity (this takes practice). Allowing yourself to feel emotional discomfort instead of trying to avoid or immediately alleviate distress can serve as your compassionate, prayerful affirmation that God is present in all reality, not only in the pleasant parts.

Perhaps you've learned that escapist behaviors like substance abuse, binge eating, and excessive sleeping may initially seem to offer distress relief, but actually cause harm and lead to further distress. This Lent may contain your invitation to break an escapist habit one day at a time, with the help of a clinical professional and/or recovery community.

This sacred season in arid territory may be bringing home to you a truth: coming closer to God often involves welcoming, with a permeable heart and an outstretched hand, a person in distress. Your compassion won't wash away the distress; you can't bring a summer rainstorm to the scorched earth. But your past experience with weakness and thirst, your subsequent healing and transformation by grace that you did nothing to generate, may contain a summons. Consider the question: What person in distress, what parched soul in search of the desert's hidden waters may you be called to accompany because you're capable of doing so? If you've been helped through the desert and you know where its aloes grow, now may be your time to lend your support to some parched, sunburned child of God.

Shelter your people, O God.
Look after animals who dwell
in burrows and branches, exposed
to a too-warm, changing climate.
Shield with gentle, cooling shadows
the ones who live in the streets,
bypassed and distressed. Surround
with tender protection the people
whose skin has been thinned
by inadequate nurture and daily cruelties
that accumulate and scrape away the scabs
before a scar can form.
Soothe all hurts, all wounded hearts
with the medicines your creation generates.
Be who you are,
God of green leaves, God of regrowth,
and help me, help us all flourish and care
for each other.
Amen.

Tuesday of Week 3

Serene Acceptance

And he said, "Truly I tell you, no prophet is accepted in the prophet's hometown."

—Luke 4:24

I created you to be fully yourself. Opponents, some yelling and telling you you're wrong, disappointing, unacceptable, or worse, may try to reduce you to less than you are. Spend your whole life, if you must, resisting their lies. Live holy and large; you're made in my image, and I proclaim you freed.

"I am no longer accepting the things I cannot change. I am changing the things I cannot accept." Attributed to social justice activist Angela Davis, these words rework the Serenity Prayer composed by Reinhold Niebuhr, a version of which people in 12-step recovery groups regularly pray. It asks God to "grant me the serenity to accept the things I cannot change, courage to change the things I can, and wisdom to know the difference."

Which do you prefer? The activist's bold self-assertion or the theologian's devout and humble request? Your answer may depend not only on your spiritual orientation, but also on the challenges at hand. Struggling to dismantle unacceptable conditions such as systems of oppression is more faithful to God revealed in Jesus than serenely accepting those conditions and calling them unchangeable.

I admire the pithy chutzpah of Davis's words, but I prefer Niebuhr's concise yet complex expression of faith. The capacity for acceptance that the Serenity Prayer asks of God makes it possible to act on those other divinely given gifts: courage, wisdom, and discernment. These stem from the serene acceptance of reality, not to be mistaken for helpless surrender. Serene acceptance can be imaged as a peaceful warrior. She knows when to save her strength and how to disarm her opponents without harming them.

The very thought of opponents may distress you. Opposition implies conflict. Maybe you strive for serenity by avoiding conflict, seeking points of agreement with others, consensus-building, or side-stepping controversial topics.

As expressed in that chestnut of a hymn, "Blest Be the Tie That Binds," "the fellowship of kindred minds is like to that above"—when you can find it.[1] But even in church (some would say especially in church), you can't always find kindred minds. After all, it was while teaching his followers how to deal with a church member who had sinned against them that Jesus promised, "For where two or three are gathered in my name, I am there among them" (Matt. 18:20). No church, no family, no life is conflict-free. A more productive question than "How can I avoid conflict?" is "How can I accept inevitable conflict and work toward its constructive resolution?" Learning to accept that conflict happens even in the faith community can foster the serenity needed to resolve conflicted situations.

The hardest conflict you face may be the struggle to accept the distressing fact that some people cannot accept *you* and indeed openly oppose you. Jesus faced such struggles. Opponents ranging from his own relations to religious leaders frequently told him, *You can't do that, you can't say that, you can't be that.* As John's Gospel puts it, "He came to what was his own, and his own people did not accept him" (1:11). Surely Jesus' many dealings with oppositional people required him to seek from God a deeper tranquility than others' affection or agreeability could bring.

Your serenity depends not on pleasing people, but on living with integrity, true to your identity and values. It's also crucial to have friends who celebrate and support you. If you're in a season of interpersonal conflict, make a point of spending time with people who accept and love you exactly as you are.

Imagine how much harder Jesus' ministry would have been had he not had a circle of close friends. No, they didn't always understand him. One or two openly opposed him (with disastrous consequences, in Judas's case). But many times, Jesus' friends came alongside him, shared meals with him, and supported his ministry at great cost to themselves. These friendships must have made bearable the times when Jesus faced severe opposition, as he did when he visited his hometown.

According to Luke, as soon as Jesus had completed his forty-day period in the desert preparing for ministry, he went back to Nazareth. In the synagogue there, among his longtime neighbors, Jesus read from the scroll of the prophet Isaiah, revealing his own anointed calling to bring good news to the poor.

You might think this proclamation would have come as good news to the locals, who were most likely living hand-to-mouth. But those who could only think of Jesus as Joseph's now-arrogant, grown-up kid found his Spirit-filled serenity and prophetic confidence unacceptable. All it took was for Jesus to say a few more provocative words for the people to become collectively enraged. Then they made a scapegoating move: they drove him out of town and tried to force him off a cliff.

This outrageously violent turn of events dramatizes the psychological cruelty that unhealthy congregations sometimes inflict on faithful disrupters in their midst. Scapegoaters operate on the mad assumption that banishing and destroying a truth-teller will restore their unchallenged serenity and power. It will not, and for the Nazareth congregation, it did not. Distress and small-minded egoism got the better of the residents. Jesus was the best thing ever to come out of their town or back to it, but to their detriment, they hated him for it.

The Nazarenes would have been profoundly better off accepting Jesus as the Anointed One he was, changing their lives according to his teachings, and celebrating gratefully the good news he proclaimed. They didn't accept Jesus and they didn't change. But you and I can. That's what Lent is all about.

God, give me the equanimity
to accept Jesus at his most challenging,
the humility to be transformed by his grace,
and the discernment to live with compassion
toward myself and others.
Amen.

Wednesday of Week 3

Radical Acceptance

> Do not be conformed to this world, but be transformed by
> the renewing of your minds, so that you may discern what is
> the will of God—what is good and acceptable and perfect.
>
> —Romans 12:2

*I have made you good, acceptable, and perfect. With you, my
beloved, I am well pleased.*

"How to get through a life that's not the life you want . . . starts with
radical acceptance."[1] Marsha Linehan, who spoke these words, lived a
life far from the life she wanted. In young adulthood, suicidal, she was
diagnosed with schizophrenia. Her barren desert consisted of an isolation room in a mental hospital. The room contained no sharp objects,
only a bed, a chair, and a small, barred window. Confinement didn't
keep Marsha from trying to end her life. She beat her head against the
walls and floor. Doctors treated her with heavy antipsychotic drugs
and electro-convulsive therapy. In her memoir *Building a Life Worth
Living*, Linehan describes herself at this time as "living in hell." She
vowed to God that one day, she would help others who were simi-
larly suffering get out of hell.

It's a vow she eventually kept, with difficulty, determination, and
divine assistance. In her early twenties, she managed to rent a room
to live in, get a job, and take night classes. She would often pray in
the chapel of a local retreat center connected to a women's religious

community. It was there, where she sat in solitary contemplation, that God's all-encompassing compassion overcame Marsha Linehan's psychic agony and self-destructive urges. She experienced a spiritual vision, a shining golden presence that led her to realize she loved herself.

Eventually, she earned a Ph.D. in psychology and a university faculty appointment. Her widely respected approach to treating people with personality disorders experiencing psychological anguish is called Dialectical Behavioral Therapy or DBT. A dialectic, as Jillian Glasgow points out, "is when two seemingly conflicting things are true at the same time. For example, 'It's snowing and it is spring.'"[2]

The dialectical part of DBT involves synthesizing, or integrating, these two seeming opposites: acceptance and change. Influenced by Zen Buddhist teachings on radical acceptance, DBT practitioners help their clients accept reality as it is and change their behaviors in healthy ways.

When, through prayer, Marsha Linehan realized she loved herself, she radically (utterly) accepted herself as loveable, *as is*. From this basis of divinely guided self-acceptance, she proceeded to live in ways that were no longer self-destructive but self-affirming. She built a life worth living by helping others get out of hell and build their own worthy, livable lives. For many people who have experienced extreme distress intolerance to the point of self-harm (on the mistaken belief that it would alleviate their suffering), Linehan's psychological research and practice have proven lifesaving.

The dialectic of acceptance and change and the capacity to hold these two seeming contradictions in creative tension are of potential value to anyone who is distressed. Hard realities of the present age—climate change, political polarization, systemic racism, and the society-wide increase in mental unhealth, to name a few—mean that everyone is susceptible to deeper-than-normal daily distress. Distress becomes suffering when viewed as unacceptable and treated as something to be escaped or combated rather than tolerated and transformed.

Let me give you a personal example of distress eventually tolerated and transformed. My (now deceased) father was an active alcoholic whose disease caused instability and turmoil in the family. At age fourteen, I was subjected to the unconscious yet powerful scapegoating mechanism common in dysfunctional families. I was made the "identified patient" and forcibly admitted to the locked psychiatric unit of a hospital despite the lack of any diagnostic evidence that I belonged among people suffering from psychosis and suicidal impulses. I had no choice but to remain hospitalized for seven weeks. Upon my release, the parenting I received did not improve, but worsened.

These facts of my personal history were hard for me to accept. At times, I tried to combat the fact of my emotional wounding by adults ill-equipped to cope with their own wounds and responsibilities. I raged and blamed those who pathologized and shamed me. Doing so didn't alleviate my pain but turned it into suffering.

Suffering arises from maladaptive reactions to pain, as when young, emotionally agonized Marsha Linehan beat her head against a wall to relieve her anguish, only to intensify it. What she mercifully came to understand through prayer was that even in her torment, she was loved and worthy.

Through my own contemplative pursuit of personal healing and wholeness, I came gradually to understand this: the mistreatment I undeservedly suffered warranted sorrow and anger. Expressing these feelings to a compassionate helper is transformative; compassion helps me move toward acceptance. Accepting the unchangeably painful facts of my personal history frees me from fruitlessly combatting them. I am free at this and any moment to choose my behavior. I can choose not to live in reaction to the wounding I once experienced. I can choose to move forward with hope, mindful of the past but not captivated by it.

I can choose to do what I'm doing now: express self-compassion in the form of honest devotional writing that I hope will bless you. I offer you today's reflection and this whole book of devotions for the Lenten journey because you may be dwelling in your own desert, your own seeming "isolation room," a hell you would never choose, and you could benefit from some compassionate company. You may be dedicated to helping yourself and other people get out of hell. I'm dedicated to helping you.

You are loved, exactly as you are. You are encompassed by the same golden, holy presence as Marsha Linehan experienced in the chapel where she knew her life was redeemed. Your life, too—every unchangeable aspect of its past and every free moment of its present—is redeemed. *You are life, and you are worth living.*

Alleluia, Light of the World.
Thank you for giving me this life
worth living.
Amen.

Thursday of Week 3

Art of Compassion

Then Jesus went with them to a place called Gethsemane; and he said to his disciples, "Sit here while I go over there and pray." He took with him Peter and the two sons of Zebedee, and began to be grieved and agitated. Then he said to them, "I am deeply grieved, even to death; remain here, and stay awake with me."

—Matthew 26:36–38

All I ask for is your wakeful presence. You cannot relieve my spirit of my fear, nor bear the grief that's mine alone. Sit, bearing witness, keeping vigil. Stay a safe distance from me, but pray. Will you do this much? I have never demanded the impossible of you.

In English, Felix Lucero's name meant "Happy Light." In childhood and in his late years, he may have attained luminous happiness, but in between, he was wounded by warfare and poverty.

Born in 1895 in Trinidad, Colorado, Lucero was Native American, possibly descended from Jicarilla Apache people (relatively little is known about his early life or ancestry). During World War I, Lucero lay gravely injured in a battlefield trench in France. He begged God to let him live, promising to devote his artistic abilities to creating religious sculpture.

After the war ended in 1918, Lucero returned to the United States, eventually becoming homeless. He arrived in Tucson, Arizona in 1938.

As unhoused people still do in this desert city, he took up residence in a makeshift shack under a bridge near the Santa Cruz riverbed. There Lucero continued his vowed, devotional artistry, sculpting biblical figures from plaster, sand, and scrap metal—any materials he could scavenge.

In 1939, the Catholic Action League of Arizona, a socially concerned organization of religious laypeople, commissioned Lucero to sculpt life-size Stations of the Cross for exhibit at the Shrine of St. Joseph of the Mountains near the Yarnell community. Several years later, Lucero sculpted the multiple depictions of Jesus, his family, his disciples, and his betrayers displayed at what is now the Garden of Gethsemane in Tucson's Felix Lucero Park. An engraved informational plaque at the park says, "Heartbreak and pain walked with the artist during his sacred efforts. . . . The work, started in 1945, continues to survive the ravages of time, floods, and many acts of vandalism."

Although olive trees grow well in Tucson, none are planted in this park. That's ironic, because *Gethsemane* is derived from *Gaḏ-Šmānê*, which in Aramaic, the language Jesus spoke, means "oil press" and refers to the oil-bearing olives that grew plentifully in the garden where Jesus prayed in deep distress before he was arrested.

By law in Pima County (where Tucson is located), for reasons of pollen control, "no . . . olive tree shall be planted; . . . the planting of a[n] . . . olive tree in the county shall constitute a nuisance."[1] Journalist Mort Rosenblum, whose publications include *Olives: The Life and Lore of a Noble Fruit*, argues that it's time to reverse this anti-olive tree legislation. In an editorial article claiming that tree species native to the Sonoran Desert, such as the Mesquite and Palo Verde, pose a greater pollen nuisance than olive trees, Rosenblum wrote, "The [Pima County] Board of Supervisors, headed by a transplanted Texan with serious allergies, outlawed the olive in the early 1980s."[2]

Some thirty years earlier, the people who built the Tucson house I share with my husband Ken planted an olive tree in the backyard, when it was still legal to do so. We cherish the shade of its silvery-leaved branches and hope someday to press oil from its dark fruit. This mature, bent-limbed tree resembles those I've seen in photos of Jerusalem's Garden of Gethsemane, a sacred site at the foot of the Mount of Olives.

There, as the reading from Matthew that opens today's reflection illustrates, Jesus, deeply distressed, retreated from his disciples to pray alone after sharing a last Passover supper with them. It's fair to apply to Jesus in this scene the words that describe sculptor Felix Lucero's experience: "Heartbreak and pain walked with the artist during his sacred efforts." Jesus' artistry was his co-creation, with his Abba-Father and the Holy Spirit, of a beautifully integrated life. Jesus sculpted his life using various holy materials: courage and compassion, solitude and service, prayer and prophecy, teaching and healing, bread and wine, body and blood.

Countless people have tried to imitate Jesus' artistry. No one could ever perfectly replicate his masterpiece of a God-centered, self-giving, world-saving life, the ultimate cost of which he realized at Gethsemane. Jesus' heartbreak and pain in the garden grew deeper when he discovered that his disciples had failed to fulfill his request for their vigilant compassion. "Stay awake with me," he had asked, but they didn't. They couldn't tolerate witnessing his distress or feeling their own, so they escaped into unconsciousness, fulfilling Jesus' tragic prediction, "You will all become deserters because of me this night" (Matt. 26:31).

Sometimes, distressed people create a desert of abandonment where others find themselves friendless and alone. But sometimes, people stay faithfully awake to their companions and callings. Delores Lucero, the wife of sacred sculptor Felix Lucero, lived such a life. Her name (literally, "Sorrow's Light") was a poetic synonym for compassion. Her grandson Don Page wrote of her, "She helped him with his art. After his death she was the one that personally cared for the garden and statues. I still remember helping my grandmother maintain the area before the City of Tucson made it a park. . . . I don't live in Tucson now but whenever I visit I go to the garden and remember my grandmother."[3]

Go to the garden. As a hymn lyrically urges, "Your Redeemer's conflict see; watch with him one bitter hour; turn not from his griefs away; learn of Jesus Christ to pray."[4]

Lord, teach me to see, watch, stay awake,
and pray with you.
Amen.

Friday of Week 3

Compassion for Fatigued Disciples

> Then he came to the disciples and found them sleeping; and he said to Peter, "So, could you not stay awake with me one hour? Stay awake and pray that you may not come into the time of trial; the spirit indeed is willing, but the flesh is weak." Again he went away for the second time and prayed, "My Father, if this cannot pass unless I drink it, your will be done." Again he came and found them sleeping, for their eyes were heavy.
>
> —Matthew 26:40–43

Rest, my beloved. Let yourself be. Lean back on me and take your rest.

Could it be that Peter, James, and John, the heavy-eyed disciples, didn't stay awake with Jesus during his distressing Gethsemane hour because they suffered from burnout? Consider Matthew's Gospel, from which today's opening Scripture comes, and you may see why I think the disciples had become burned out—exhausted and withdrawn.

Jesus had dispatched his disciples to do demanding work: "Cure the sick, raise the dead, cleanse the lepers, cast out demons," all "without payment" (10:8). When traveling with Jesus, the disciples subsisted on raw grain they picked themselves, while religious fundamentalists looked askance at them (12:1–2). The disciples faced hungry crowds in the desert and mountains (14:13–16; 15:33), and rough weather at sea (14:24). When they struggled to understand Jesus' difficult teachings, they also had to cope with his harsh reactions (16:11, 23). They experienced mystical visions but also ministry failures (17:2, 16).

Perhaps you hear, as I do, fatigue and fear in Peter's words to Jesus: "Look, we have left everything and followed you. What then will we have?" (19:27). The disciples followed Jesus into Jerusalem, where his prophetic rhetoric intensified tensions (chap. 23) until he was finally arrested. At this point in the Gospel, Matthew bluntly narrates the fulfillment of Jesus' earlier prediction: "Then all the disciples deserted him and fled" (26:56).

Their inability to stay awake and their desertion of Jesus suggest to me that the disciples were suffering from conditions that present-day clinicians call empathic distress, burnout, and compassion fatigue. All three terms warrant explanation.

According to clinical pharmacologist Trisha Dowling, "empathic distress . . . is the strong aversive and self-oriented response to the suffering of others, accompanied by the desire to withdraw from a situation in order to protect oneself from excessive negative feelings."[1] This applies to the disciples. They could not tolerate their own distress upon witnessing Jesus' suffering, so they withdrew from him by sleeping and running away.

The disciples appear to have traveled, worked, served, and exercised their authority to heal emotionally disturbed people and "cure every disease and every sickness," to the depletion of their own spirits and the exhaustion of their own emotional resources (Matt. 10:1). I believe they suffered from the burnout that stems from empathic distress, the steep cost of feeling others' pain. (It's worth noting that especially for health workers, burnout is a significant occupational hazard listed in the "International Classification of Diseases 11th Revision.") Over the course of their caring ministry, the disciples probably absorbed more of their hungry, ailing, impoverished neighbors' suffering than they could handle. Such "empathic distress. . .leads to burnout, characterized as emotional exhaustion, withdrawal, depersonalization, and a decreased sense of personal accomplishment."[2]

Burnout is sometimes viewed as synonymous with "compassion fatigue," a phrase coined in 1992 by Carla Joinson, RN. It has gained widespread use, particularly because of the global pandemic's crushing effects on health care workers. Merriam-Webster defines compassion fatigue as "the physical and mental exhaustion and emotional withdrawal experienced by those who care for sick or traumatized people over an extended period of time."[3]

Dowling argues, however, that "compassion does not fatigue." As you might expect of a pharmacologist, she cites neurochemical data to make the point that compassion doesn't wear out caregivers, empathy does. In the human brain, empathy—experiencing others' pain—depletes dopamine, the so-called feel-good neurotransmitter. But compassion is different. Grounded in positive concern and the motivation to relieve suffering, compassion does not deplete dopamine, but stimulates its practitioner's brain in rewarding, uplifting ways. Therefore, Dowling exultantly claims, "Compassion does not fatigue—it is neurologically rejuvenating!"[4]

It seems the depleted disciples, who crashed out a stone's throw from an agonized Jesus, then abandoned him at the moment of his arrest, hadn't learned the difference between experiencing others' pain to their own detriment and caring for others to everyone's benefit. They were so worn out they had no compassion to offer Jesus when he desperately needed it.

Maybe you've come to a comparable low point in your own life. As a pastor and as a daughter of an aging parent, I sometimes confront my limited ability to care for others in distress. I know what it is to become emotionally and spiritually depleted. It takes intention and practice to move from vicarious suffering to healthy compassion. The move is possible to make, and Lent is a fine season in which to make it. In tomorrow's reflection, I'll offer you some insights, derived from evidence-based compassion training and contemplative wisdom, on avoiding empathic distress and the burnout it can cause.

Today, I encourage you to reflect compassionately on the image of those sleeping, then fleeing, disciples of Jesus. Christians all too commonly condemn them, ourselves, and each other for the vulnerable facts of our God-given humanity. We are fragile and finite, sometimes fatigued and frightened people. Our spirits may indeed be willing to offer compassion, but our flesh is weak. We need and we are given compassion, as the risen Jesus' ultimate words to the disciples make clear. Although they had abandoned him, he offered them—and he offers everyone—his abiding presence: "And remember," he said, "I am with you always, to the end of the age" (Matt. 28:20).

I need not ask you, Jesus,
to be with me
because you always are.
Nothing I have done
or failed to do can banish you.
I let myself lean back,
restful in your presence.
By your grace,
grant me peace.
Amen.

Saturday of Week 3

Compassion Training

> Now, discipline always seems painful rather than pleasant at the time, but later it yields the peaceful fruit of righteousness to those who have been trained by it.
> —Hebrews 12:11

You are my precious child and I nurture you toward full maturity. Everyone you meet is a teacher sent to foster your loving-kindness for all beings. Exercise and strengthen your mind; think humbly, reflect gratefully. Know your thoughts. Be still and know me.

The writer of the Letter to the Hebrews, quoted above, makes discipline sound punitive. If you read Hebrews 12:11 in context in a standard translation of the Bible, you'll see the theme of punishment, with God depicted as a loving punisher. This is problematic theology. Many people have suffered wounding by faith communities and families who exercised discipline abusively in God's name.

Sometimes, theologically troubling Scriptures can be helpfully rethought. For example, in its original Greek, the word translated as *discipline* in the verse from Hebrews refers to childrearing. *Training,* rooted in a word related to *gymnasium,* refers to exertion and exercise. *Righteousness* refers to justice that God brings about. Although the Scripture writer had stern linguistic and theological intentions, none of the Greek terms the writer used is necessarily punitive or violent, as Eugene Peterson's creative interpretation of Hebrews 12 demonstrates:

God is educating you . . . treating you as dear children. This trouble you're in isn't punishment; it's training. . . . Why not embrace God's training so we can truly live? . . . God is doing what is best for us, training us to live God's holy best. At the time, discipline isn't much fun. It always feels like it's going against the grain. Later, of course, it pays off big-time, for it's the well-trained who find themselves mature in their relationship with God.[1]

Can you imagine a scenario in which you would "embrace God's training," develop practical compassion skills, and thereby "mature in relationship with God," the source of all compassion? Can you imagine such a scenario taking place at church?

A church that doesn't emphasize spirituality and spiritual practice can look like a barren desert to you if you're seeking formation and training in the art of prayerful loving-kindness. Despite Jesus' compassion for people who faced hunger, disease, oppression, and poverty, compassion as a Christian practice is rarely emphasized in the traditional faith-formation language of the church.

Andrew Dreitcer, co-director of the Center for Engaged Compassion, claims "there are no classical or traditional Christian practices that have been specifically identified or named as compassion-formation practices."[2] Nevertheless, Christian tradition is rich with wisdom by which "to live God's holy best." Dreitcer points out that "compassion-formation lies at the heart of virtually all Christian spiritual practices."[3] From private prayer to public worship, from acts of community service to faith-based social justice movements, the whole of Christian life sings, "Lord, make us more loving."[4]

By God, you can be made more healthily loving. Compassion is a skill you can learn and practice through compassion-formative disciplines of mind and heart. Compassion training can equip you to increase your self-awareness, respond with care to people in distress (including yourself), reduce the likelihood that you'll burn out doing so, and increase the possibility of your yielding "the peaceful fruit of righteousness."

Books like Andrew Dreitcer's *Living Compassion* and Joyce Rupp's *Boundless Compassion* emphasize a Christian approach while insights from nonreligious fields complement such spiritual resources. Nonsectarian centers for the study and practice of compassion are emerging in the United States. In the Desert Southwest, for example, the University of Arizona is home to the Center for Compassion Studies. There, researchers, students, and community members "explore the belief that the potential to develop compassion exists in every person, and that it is a quality that can be deliberately expanded and deepened through training, often with great benefits to the individual as well as society at large."[5]

The physical sciences and global spiritual traditions inform compassion practices that guard against empathic distress, the emotional exhaustion caused by feeling others' suffering. Neurobiologists Tania Singer and Olga Klimecki have found that compassion training "not only promotes prosocial behavior, but also augments positive affect and resilience, which in turn fosters better coping with stressful situations."[6] Compassion training sometimes involves the adaptation of a Tibetan Buddhist mental discipline called *lojong* and a compassion-meditative practice called *metta,* which has Buddhist, Hindu, and Jain origins. To practice *metta,* you sequentially recall a loved one, yourself, a person about whom you feel neutrally, an enemy, and finally humankind entirely, bidding compassion to each and all.

Michael Dowling is a pastor who has adapted *metta* as an "altruism and compassion meditation" for use in a Christian context. Early in Dowling's meditation guidelines, the practitioner is asked, "What is your motivation in meditating? Is it for your benefit only, or is it directed to the benefit of all beings and to the glory of God? Is your focus and caring limited and narrow, or is it held in the vastness of God's love?"[7]

In his book *Blessed Relief: What Christians Can Learn from Buddhists about Suffering,* Episcopal priest and psychotherapist Gordon Peerman offers guidelines for a *metta*-inspired, meditative "Compassion Practice." I'll conclude today's reflection with a prayer of my composing prompted by Peerman's guidelines. I encourage you to still yourself and adopt a prayerful attitude. Then, reading the words below, mindfully extend God's compassion toward a loved one, toward a person who has helped you whose own need for help now concerns you, toward someone you don't know, toward an enemy, toward yourself, and finally, toward all beings. Consider continuing this meditative prayer practice daily for the remainder of Lent. The discipline may help train you to regard all beings with compassion and cause your relationship with God to ripen into greater maturity and fruitfulness.

Source of all serenity, still my mind and body.
Help me accept this moment as it is, without resisting it.
In this body, created in your image, I notice sensations.
I allow feelings to rise and fall away.
I receive and return your gift of breath, your Spirit.
I receive it and return it, receive it and return it gratefully.

To the loved one on my mind,
bring freedom from suffering, bring happiness.

To someone who has helped me who now needs help,
bring freedom from suffering, bring happiness.

To someone whose suffering is unknown to me but known to you,
God of mercy, bring freedom from suffering, bring happiness.

And yes, to one whom I have called my enemy,
whose harmful actions I have struggled to forgive,
God of limitless compassion, bring freedom from suffering,
bring happiness.

To me, to my life, my breath and body, my whole being,
Creator, bring liberty from suffering, bring joy.
Let compassion flow through me to encompass
every being in your good Creation.

By the power of your loving-kindness, God of all,
free all beings from suffering.
Lead your world to wholeness, happiness, and peace.
Amen.

Week 4

Your Whole Mind

Sabbath Rest Stop

When I was twenty-three, I was baptized. Before that, I'd had no Christian education or spiritual formation, no religious history to later build on or recover from. To try to establish a biblical foundation for my faith, I attended a Kerygma Bible study class. I carried a hefty three-ring binder full of lessons to a fancy downtown church and sat in a classroom where an instructor droned through the curriculum. I got the impression that the Bible contained no good news, no juicy stories, no impassioned poetry, nothing to stimulate a deeply felt relationship with God or move my mind from content comprehension to prayer. I soon dropped out of the class and started attending worship at a less fancy, funkier church in another neighborhood.

I loved it there. The people were warm, smart, and actively committed to social justice. And I was puzzled because I couldn't tell what inspired their demonstrated care for neighbors and their dedication to dismantling oppressive social systems. My spiritual siblings in this congregation were compassionate, but why? What, or who, was moving them to spend overnights welcoming guests to the church's homeless shelter or striving to overcome their church denomination's then-exclusive, antigay ordination standards? What stimulated these Christians to alleviate human suffering? I can't know what was going on in their souls, but the fact that many of them were queer and therefore (outside our congregation) were frequently othered and treated as defective and unwelcome surely sensitized them to injustice and mobilized their ministries of extravagant welcome.

Certainly, they welcomed me as I was, an emerging contemplative in search of spiritual formation beyond what a small, urban, activist congregation could be expected to provide. I was unacquainted with the contemplative branches of Christian tradition (I eventually discovered these, thankfully, among Benedictines and other prayer-centered people). At the time, I pressed on as best I could, enrolling in a theological seminary. Naively perhaps, I hoped that doing so would heal within me the wounds that prior years of spiritual deprivation had caused. More than soul-fed, seminary enriched me intellectually and prepared me vocationally. I earned academic degrees in theological studies and divinity.

The habits of critical inquiry, analysis, and interpretation that I learned have proven useful in my pastoral and expressive work. The life of the mind isn't everything, but it's a major part of a meaningful existence. Paying attention, deepening awareness, reflecting on experience, and seeking insight from teachers and traditions all make for an understanding, mindful life. Mindful practices of thought as well as prayer are crucial to cultivating compassion. On the face of it, compassion may seem to emerge purely from sentiments like sorrow and affection. While emotion does play a key role in cultivating care that alleviates suffering in self and others, so also does mental discipline factor in importantly. Mental attunement, sound information, clear analysis, self-knowledge, and realistic reasoning all play key roles in a life of faith that's motivated more by authentic compassion than by the compulsion to judge and fix people according to my big ideas.

This week's reflections will focus on the mind. I'll encourage you to consider what it can mean to love God "with all your mind." Jesus, invoking an essential teaching from the Torah, commanded his disciples to love God all-mindfully (Deut. 6:4–7; Matt. 22:37–40; Mark 12:30–31; Luke 10:27). All-mindful love may entail rational rigor, but if it's to engender compassion that alleviates suffering, it's also got to engage the imagination, awaken curiosity, excite, change, and discipline a learner's mind, sometimes through contemplative practice.

The life of the mind, lived to the glory of God for your own good and the benefit of others, is a life worth living. Practicing all-mindful love can deepen your awareness of suffering's causes, inform your efforts to alleviate it, and protect you from suffering unduly in the process. This week, I invite you to dwell with me in the desert of the mind, the place of inner stillness and attention where it's possible to notice both destructive and constructive thoughts and learn to navigate them. The actual Egyptian desert served as an earthen temple for Christian contemplatives of the fourth and fifth centuries. From them people of faith continue to learn mindful, prayerful habits that foster the God-centered, humble compassion to which Jesus devoted his life. Today, may you devote yourself to a restorative Sabbath through worship, play, and rest. Tomorrow, I'll introduce you to a mindful Christian of the ancient desert.

Monday of Week 4

A Desert Mentor

But he turned and said to Peter, "Get behind me, Satan! You are a stumbling block to me; for you are setting your mind not on divine things but on human things."

—Matthew 16:23

The Holy Spirit takes compassion on our weakness, and though we are impure he often comes to visit us. If he should find our spirit praying to him out of love for truth he then descends upon it and dispels the whole army of thoughts and reasonings that beset it. And too he urges it on to the works of spiritual prayer.

—Evagrius Ponticus[1]

My thoughts are not your thoughts, but I see you striving to align yours with mine, and I am pleased. Set your mind on me and learn my ways. Seek exemplars and guides, mentors in the contemplative way. Follow them into the desert of prayer. Let my Spirit visit you there and lead you to compassionate insight.

The year 380 CE was a heated, heady time theologically, especially in Constantinople, the Roman imperial capitol. The Christian church had been considered legitimate for fewer than seventy years. The New Testament was still, in a sense, a work in progress—written, but not yet formally, finally canonized. Interpretation of the Bible was a matter of sometimes violent conflict. Street fights broke out over questions of faith. Did God have a physical body or not? Had God created Jesus, or had Jesus been born as God's only son?

A well-connected church professional named Evagrius arrived on the scene. Thirty-three years old, brainy, and brokenhearted over the sudden death of his mentor, Basil, the Bishop of Caesarea Mazaca, Evagrius had skipped out of Caesarea without so much as saying goodbye to his friends. Maybe he was trying to outrun his grief. Maybe he was looking for a new mentor.

Evagrius loved a theological conflict. But he wielded words, not brickbats, "inveighing against every heresy with hot-headed homilies," according to his fifth-century biographer and disciple, Palladius.[2]

Evagrius' passions sometimes got the better of him. While climbing the church leadership ladder and living a high life, he had an affair with a woman who was married to a nobleman. To invoke the words of Jesus that open today's reflection, Evagrius was setting his mind not on divine things but on such human things as sexual conquest and careerism. One night, an alarming dream made him realize he was putting his spiritual integrity and safety at risk. Intent on reforming his life and rededicating himself to God, he set out for Jerusalem. There he came under the spiritual care of a devout woman named Melania, who counseled him to seek God through a contemplative life in the desert.

The desert spirituality that Evagrius eventually entered Egypt to practice was co-created by Mediterranean women and men of the fourth century who were hungry for God and skeptical of institutional religion. They looked at the mayhem and glitz of the imperial church and said, *No, thanks. If that's official Christianity, give me something simpler yet harder, closer to the life of prayer and wisdom, courage and compassion that Jesus lived.* They left cities and towns and migrated to the Nile River Valley. Some practiced radical solitude while others lived communally. Hundreds, even thousands of people formed this monastic movement, convinced God was calling them to practice simplicity, self-awareness, and devotional discipline that would lead them to deepened holiness and loving-kindness. Eventually, Evagrius became a prominent figure among these Desert Mothers and Fathers.

He was a contemplative theologian and spiritual director, a disciplined writer and sacred psychologist of the ancient world. I introduce Evagrius to you because his life involved the kinds of challenges and growth that spiritual seekers still care about. His writings about mindful, prayerful practices read like the insights of a person who has faced his demons and can help others wrestle with theirs. He was smart, articulate, and deeply versed in Scripture. Although some of his writings deal systematically with the human mind, it's ultimately the mind of God that interested him.

Evagrius' mystical relationship with divinity was forged in the fires of his humanity—his heartaches, ambitions, erotic longings, failures, and fears. Eventually, he sacrificed everything that kept him from becoming a mindful, compassionate person of faith. Because the sacrifice didn't come easily, because he confronted his own vulnerability and counseled others dealing with theirs, his understandings of the human mind and heart ring true.

Evagrius and other Desert Christians of the ancient world can teach present-day people a lot about ourselves—who we are, what we think, how our thoughts can get us into trouble, and how divine power greater than our own can lead us toward wisdom, compassion, and peace. If you enjoy connecting the lessons of antiquity with your pursuit of a God-mindful life, you might benefit from reading the sayings and stories of the Desert Mothers and Fathers.

Be mindful of me, loving God.
Help me trust that I am ever on your mind.
Help me relinquish all anxiety.
I aspire to look upon myself and all people
as you look upon creation,
not with condemnation
but with insight and consoling mercy.
Foster my awareness that my quest
for Christlike compassion
is neither new nor mine alone.
For my forebears in faith
who gave up privilege and power
to seek you in the desert
and learn your all-embracing love, I thank you.
Counselor of the troubled,
Comforter of hurting souls,
Teacher of all searchers,
cultivate in me the mind of Christ.
Amen.

Tuesday of Week 4

Mindful Resistance

But take care and watch yourselves closely, so as neither to forget the things that your eyes have seen nor to let them slip from your mind all the days of your life.

—Deuteronomy 4:9a

I am mindful of you always, as I also remember your fore-bears. No one is forgotten, nothing is lost. Though the clay tablets that bore my inscribed Commandments turned to dust ages ago, their wisdom is etched on your conscience, as it was written in the minds of those who went before you. Remember them, remember me.

One July, I set out from my desert home to take a class at St. John's University in Collegeville, Minnesota. What blessed relief from the searing Sonoran heat it was to walk the grassy, lakeside campus, under the fragrant shade of old-growth pines and conifers. Yet I carried the desert within me and drew on its familiar, blazing feel in a class called "Passions and Prayer." Our teacher was Columba Stewart, OSB, a brilliant yet humble monastic scholar. He introduced the students to ancient Desert Christians' ways of thinking about the mind and prayer-fully dealing with passions. We learned that the ancients employed their rational faculties to manage irrational impulses.

Yesterday, I introduced you to Evagrius, a Desert Christian whose psychologically insightful spirituality, Stewart taught us, dealt with

101

the interplay of desire and resistance. What a Lenten tension that is: the allure of the things you want versus the self-restraint that a God-centered life necessitates.

Think of the Ten Commandments. Nine of them mandate practical resistance to damaging impulses. Acted on, the desires to overwork, annihilate enemies, violate covenants, steal property, and tell lies can destroy lives, relationships, and communities. Resistance is required. In the book of Deuteronomy (quoted at the opening of today's reflection), Moses urges his listeners to practice mindful resistance, to take care and watch themselves closely. Mindful resistance lays the foundation for compassion motivated by the calling to alleviate suffering, as opposed to some unacknowledged, unmet desire (for approval, power, attention, and the like).

In the desert, Evagrius developed a spirituality of mindful resistance and taught it to others. "Both anger and hatred increase anger," Evagrius wrote. "But almsgiving and meekness diminish [anger] even when it is present."[1] At the heart of anger and hatred lies a wound that can give rise to violent desire—to retaliate, dominate, and violate. Almsgiving and meekness (what you and I would call charitable giving and humility) are acts and attitudes of resistance that can redirect angry energies toward nonviolent, compassionate ends. For example, when I was angry about a U.S. president's misogyny, I channeled that energy toward constructive ends by supporting an organization that provides health care to low-income women. This was better for my neighbors and for my own mind than trying to fight oppression with contempt.

Resisting the desire to lash out in anger and redirecting anger's energy toward compassionate purposes are different from submerging emotion. All submergence does is bury the wound in the body and mind. There it festers, often causing harmful physical, mental, relational, and social effects like heart disease, depression, domestic abuse, and violent crime. Anger and painful passions need to be expressed and heard.

If, as Martin Luther King Jr. said, "a riot is the language of the unheard," then anger is the riotous community's long-unheard emotion.[2] King heard his neighbors' anger and his own. He strove to direct civil rights activists' rage toward prophetically compassionate ends: the dismantling of racist laws to alleviate Black Americans' suffering.

Nonviolent resistance in the public square can convert collective rage into social righteousness.

Social transformation is rooted not only in collective action, but more profoundly in personal transformation. Social justice activists whose fuel for the struggle is untransformed anger rarely appear to be people in good mental and spiritual health. The need for self-compassion and self-care among activists has gained serious attention. For example, Rev. Michael Moore, associate for African American Intercultural Congregational Support in the Presbyterian Church (U.S.A.), has said, "We want to encourage Black, Indigenous and People of Color with the message that we must remain resilient and resist the forces of injustice, but develop new coping skills of rest, self-care, recovery and repair for self, family, and community."[3]

Rest, self-care, recovery, and repair foster personal transformation by God, as the commandment to keep the Sabbath holy makes plain. Personal transformation is the goal to which Desert Christians like Evagrius devoted themselves. In austere landscapes, they took care, watched themselves closely, and through disciplined, prayerful resistance, sought to be changed into people like Jesus. "*Ascesis* [spiritual self-discipline] consists in keeping the commandments," Evagrius wrote. "The goal of the ascetic life is charity."[4] To put these words in the terms of this Lenten devotional, God-centered, mindful spiritual practice can help you become self-compassionate and motivated to alleviate others' suffering.

Columba Stewart exemplifies sacred self-care. His personal disciplines include regular swimming workouts and praying the Jesus Prayer (a short, meditative prayer, said repeatedly, internally, which originated among the ancient Desert Christians; its words comprise the first line of the prayer that concludes today's reflection). Although Stewart looks after himself, he also enters deeply into desert places where others suffer, sometimes at great personal risk. One prominent magazine profile put it this way: "As ISIS militants have destroyed countless artifacts, Stewart has attempted to counter them by working with Christian and Muslim communities in hotspots such as Iraq and Syria."[5] With interfaith partners, Stewart has retrieved and digitized endangered historic manuscripts like those written by Evagrius.

Today in my desert home, I remember the muggy Minnesota afternoon when I bought my paperback copy of Evagrius' *The Praktikos*

& Chapters on Prayer, now coming apart at the binding. The book is fragile but the insights it contains are robust, not soon to slip from the mind, God willing.

> *Lord, Jesus Christ, have mercy on me.*
> *Help me mind my emotions*
> *and release them well.*
> *May I become well*
> *and from my wellness,*
> *work for that of others.*
> *Amen.*

Wednesday of Week 4

How Do You Listen?

"Then pay attention to how you listen."
—Luke 8:18a

Mary . . . sat at the Lord's feet and listened to what he was saying.
—Luke 10:39b

A wind-carved canyon of ruddy rock bends through the desert, its sculptural structure reminiscent of an ear. I'm hearing you, leading you to tell me a truth I'll safekeep. Make your plea. I'm listening. I'm already answering in mercy you'll eventually perceive.

I have a friend of more than twenty years who listens, in the words of St. Benedict, "with the ear of the heart." She and I have spent many hours together, talking and listening over meals or side by side on road trips. When something is troubling me and I need a good listening-to, even if she's heard it all before, my friend lends me her ear. She listens for as long as it takes me to say what I haven't said before. Sometimes I don't know what I think until she hears me to the point of insight.

Being listened to like this feels like hiking up a narrow, shaded, tree-lined path and finally emerging into a clearing. I'm close to the bright, spacious sky now. I can see the desert valley below, where I live. From here, my concerns look less looming and consuming than they looked before. It's cooler up here. I can see distances, faraway blue mountain profiles against a paler sky. It takes me a while to catch my breath. I breathe and behold the big world and catch myself feeling untroubled. My friend only listened. Nothing has changed but my mind, yet everything seems transformed.

Two decades of friendship between simpatico women help to make possible this transformative listening. But no explanation can fully capture what happens when the ear of one heart is opened to the voice of another. It's good, this mystery of being met in one place and accompanied to a different place without ever actually climbing a mountain or shifting the car into drive.

"Pay attention to how you listen," Jesus says. If I spent my life paying attention, it would be a life well spent. Noticing matters. Focus and self-awareness, receptivity, openness to what's revealed rather than reactivity to what I think I heard—all these make the difference between attention paid and attention feigned until I get to talk again.

Do I listen to comprehend? To defend? Do I listen as well as my friend? Do I allow your words to occupy my mind even when I have my own dilemmas to attend to? Am I so absorbed in my thoughts, so sure of my opinions that I'm reluctant to set these aside and consider your story? Am I willing to suspend judgment and welcome you just as you come, unfinished, repeating yourself perhaps, but also revealing yourself, even in that? Am I so invested in my own convictions that I believe I can't afford to imagine your version of things? How do I listen?

Oh, it varies. Some days the reception is clear. The ear of my heart is attentive and ready. Other days, I listen less well because one stressor or another has me constricted, stretched, pressured, unable to take in more information or noise. Some days I struggle to make it to the day's end in one piece, in one peace. Some days I need extra silence.

Pay attention to how you listen. Attune yourself to your mind as it attends and comprehends something singly, or as it flits, fleet as a sparrow, from one bug to another. Imagine yourself in the clearing near a mountain path's summit. Catch your breath here and discern.

Do you hear your own breathing, hear this lively patch of planet humming, hear the day presenting itself without pretense or script, improvising on the spot? What if you always lived and listened like this, with nothing preconceived in mind, simply sunlit and available? How strange you would be, how holy.

Listen if you can as my friend listens, suspending judgment and the eager ego's demands, simply willing, unthreatened, to accept what's said and not said, to let it all be and let that be enough.

Could it be that Jesus needed to be listened to like this? Could it be that Mary of Bethany sitting at the Lord's feet was not only learning but also offering the ministry of listening to a man frequently misheard and misunderstood? We don't know what Jesus said that day, only that he spoke, and Mary took in his words. Her story, wedged between the parable of the prodigal and Jesus at prayer, may contain an untold narrative of Mary's compassion for Jesus. Maybe Jesus needed only one thing: to talk to a friend, to be listened to until he came to a clearing and found the better part of his life.

Sometimes when I try to pray,
I can't even hear myself think.
I can't sense you, Lord,
receiving my prayer,
and I wonder if you're there.
I'm Martha, wondering if you don't care.
I'm an anxious disciple, demanding,
Teach me to pray.
Then I remember, and I speak
the familiar petition for bread,
forgiveness, and protection from temptation
until I get to glory forever and wonder,
is this the end?
I haven't paid attention to my own prayer.
All I can do is trust that you listened,
and you'll lead me forward from this.
Amen.

Thursday of Week 4

Sing Praise with the Mind

What should I do then? I will pray with the spirit, but I will pray with the mind also; I will sing praise with the spirit, but I will sing praise with the mind also.

—1 Corinthians 14:15

Melodies rising from human hearts and throats, words of prayer and praise, repeated, repeated, remind you I am the song. I am the peace for which you long. I am with you in music and lyric, present in breath between words, alive in beauty and silence.

Icons, candlelit paintings of Jesus' placid face, held in a congregation's contemplative gaze, are surrounded by the people's rich, united voice, rising and falling in song. If you've worshiped in the Taizé style, you've prayed and sung praise in such a manner, with spirit, body, and mind. An ecumenical fraternal community in Burgundy, France, Taizé is a beloved, globally influential pilgrimage site, especially for young adults. Faith communities around the world have adopted Taizé chants.

These simple, communally sung, meditative lyrics and melodies of intuited (not pre-determined) duration, interspersed with silence, can lead you into the interior desert, the place of uncomplicated presence and holy encounter. The Taizé community says that through their songs, "our being finds an inner unity in God. [The songs] can continue in the silence of our hearts when we are at work, speaking with others or resting. . . . They allow us to keep on praying even when we are unaware of it."[1] Regular, reverent singing shapes people from within and helps them approach even their unsung tasks and challenges with love for God foremost yet effortlessly in mind.

Taizé's Swiss founder, Brother Roger Schütz, suffered from severe tuberculosis during his youth. Of that time, he wrote, "I began to realize that a God of love and compassion cannot be the author of suffering."[2] Brother Roger's father, a pastor in the Reformed tradition, wanted his only son to become a clergyman, and Brother Roger did go on to study Reformed theology. But his calling to a compassion-centered life in a religious community led him to create a place of worship and unity that grew and evolved over decades. At Taizé, monastic men dwell together in harmony. Visitors from many cultures and spiritual backgrounds sojourn and sing God's praise together in the Church of Reconciliation.

Despite what some consider to be the church's peculiar appearance (one visitor said it "looks like a 1960s aircraft hangar with onion dome attachments"[3]), many pilgrims find that praying there cultivates all-mindful, all-encompassing love for God and neighbor. Since its original construction in the mid-twentieth century, the sprawling sanctuary has undergone multiple expansions, driven by Brother Roger Schütz's passion for offering an unconditional welcome to all comers. In peak months, some 5,000 or more people gather at Taizé to pray and sing God's praise.

Imagine the tonal ocean all those blended voices co-create. Imagine the effect on the brain and mind of joining your own voice to that chorus. Such unison breathing and intoning might enable you to know, at a deeper-than-rational level, the meaning of Paul's promise to the Philippians: "And the peace of God, which surpasses all understanding, will guard your hearts and your minds in Christ Jesus" (4:7).

Researchers in the relatively new field of neurotheology have found that meditative chanting promotes measurable calming effects, improves practitioners' mental concentration and memory, and enhances their felt sense of well-being. The brain is neuroplastic, capable of changing and adapting to experience. "Our brains are continuously being sculpted, whether you like it or not, wittingly or unwittingly," says Richard Davidson, a neuroscientist who studies the brains of meditators. Findings like Davidson's seem to confirm the experience of Taizé brothers whose songs allow them "to keep on praying even when . . . unaware of it."[4] At both conscious and unconscious levels, their love for God is all-mindful because they "let the word of Christ dwell in [them] richly . . . and with gratitude in [their] hearts sing psalms, hymns, and spiritual songs to God" (Col. 3:16).

Brother Roger Schütz died in the very place where the Taizé Community sings. In 2005, at a prayer service attended by some 2,500 people in the Church of Reconciliation, a deranged person stabbed him in the throat, the body's channel of song. Although they suffered tremendous shock and grief at the death of their community's founder, the surviving brothers urged people not to condemn but to forgive his murderer, as the brothers prayed for God to do. In this, as in all their ministries, the Taizé Community realized the wisdom of words that Brother Roger had composed in a letter just hours before his death: "To the extent that the Church is able to bring healing to our hearts by communicating forgiveness and compassion, it makes a fullness of communion with Christ more accessible."[5]

What makes accessible and full your own experience of communion with Christ? What aspects of the church's ministries bring healing to your heart? As a writer and preacher whose "song" is more often spoken than sung, I find that singing with my congregation and listening to the spiritual songs of my church's choir communicate God's forgiveness and compassion to me. I'm grateful my Sunday sermons are flanked by a choral anthem and a hymn. From these songs, I draw the deep breath that equips me to preach and pray for God's people. In this Lenten season, whether through Taizé chants or other kinds of sacred music, may you hear the melodic voice of the divine and lift up your own in tuneful response. May singing in community make you mindful of God's all-encompassing mercy and move you to communicate compassion to others, even when you're unaware of doing so.

Our voices, resonant, blending,
ascending and bending
around simple, yearning words

and reassurances, convey to us
all for which we ask you:
peace
of mind and world, Lord,
peace of mind and world.
Amen.

Friday of Week 4

Sacred Self-Compassion

> Do your best to present yourself to God as one approved by him, a worker who has no need to be ashamed, rightly explaining the word of truth.
>
> 2 Timothy 2:15

Present yourself as you are: radiant. I made you to reflect my light. I am glorified not by perfection but by the genuine person. Your integrity is meant to burn bright, undiminished. Shade that ashamed, unhealed people throw your way cannot overshadow the fire I lit when I set your spirit aflame. Shine, my candle, my lamp, undampened.

The word "shame" occurs hundreds of times in the Bible. Its writers lived in ancient honor-shame cultures. People's worth and access to communal belonging were largely determined by whether their social position was deemed honorable or shameful. More than an emotionally painful experience, being shamed sometimes resulted in people's exclusion from families and communities, which led to the outcasts' material and spiritual impoverishment.

The Psalms are rife with pleas for God's protection against being put to shame. Shaming could afflict not only individuals, but also nations. Speaking ferociously against the Chaldeans, for example, the prophet Jeremiah said, "your mother shall be utterly shamed, and she who bore you shall be disgraced. Lo, she shall be the last of the nations, a wilderness, dry land, and a desert" (50:12). In this damning prophecy, the desert is not a place of divine encounter and sustenance, but of divine desertion, the direst consequence of shame.

In a Mediterranean society where threats of shame and desertion loomed large, Paul wrote refreshingly gracious words to bolster emerging pastor Timothy's spirit, saying to him, in effect, *God approves of you. You do good work. There's no need for you to be ashamed.*

The good news that Jesus proclaimed is all about people being freed by God from the burden of shame. The gospel's message was radically, religiously countercultural, and therefore required great courage on the part of its preachers, including Timothy. While many present-day readers of Paul's letters appropriately object to some of his antiquated teachings, particularly concerning women and people who were enslaved, it's nevertheless possible to appreciate Paul the mentor's encouraging message to his younger colleague: *Do your best. God approves. Be unashamed. You're telling the truth.*

Early in my theological seminary education, I compared myself unfavorably to other seminarians, concluded I wasn't pastor material, and stepped away from the ministry preparation process. I deepened my voluntary church involvement, however, which brought me such satisfaction and joy, I eventually returned to seminary. Yet when a pastor whose church I served as a seminary intern encouraged me much as Paul encouraged Timothy, I still found her affirmations hard to believe. Self-doubt was a mental habit of mine. It had more to do with the yet-unhealed emotional wounds I'd experienced early in life than with any intrinsic unfitness for ministry.

Now I know from experience that self-compassion founded on God's grace can heal disgrace, shame, and self-doubt. I did eventually become a thriving pastor and have served congregations for over two decades. Pastoring is not easy, especially in an era of church decline and ideological division. But having learned to view and treat myself with compassion akin to God's loving-kindness for all creatures, I persevere in faith and ministry and encourage others (including you) to do likewise.

You can strengthen your self-compassion through mindful, healing practices such as expressive writing, contemplative prayer, and intelligent spiritual reading. Devotedly showing yourself kindness grounded in God's love can debunk internalized lies that diminish your dignity and sense of worth. You can avail yourself of the Holy Spirit's power to help you change self-destructive thought patterns and beliefs. Your neuroplastic brain can be changed, resulting in your increased inner peace and contentment. You can become more consistently aware that you are God-beloved and blessed. Despite what you may have been told, you are inherently precious in the sight of your divine Creator. The more deeply you come to believe this, the more you can live from a center of serene, positive self-regard, able to cherish and encourage others. You can bless them simply by being yourself.

Founder of Compassion Focused Therapy and author of *The Compassionate Mind,* Paul Gilbert is a clinical psychologist whose widely respected work has done much to inspire my writing in this book. Affirming the power of self-compassion to foster people's well-being and emotional coping abilities, Gilbert points to the work of clinical psychologist Kristin Neff, author of *Self-Compassion.* Both Gilbert and Neff are influenced by Buddhist wisdom and mindfulness practices. These pose no theological or spiritual threat to Christians and in fact can meaningfully support Christian life. Even so, compassion-enhancing treasures embedded in Christian tradition, such as ancient desert monastics' contemplative teachings and practices, warrant more attention than they tend to receive outside of scholarly settings.

Jesus of Nazareth, the Christian tradition's greatest treasure, embodied God's compassion. Touching and teaching downtrodden, shame-burdened people, Jesus restored their dignity and empowered them to live wholly, as God intended. Although no longer physically walking the earth, Jesus' risen, living presence and the Holy Spirit's restorative movement enable people like you and me to claim and proclaim the same healing grace that enabled Timothy (encouraged by his mentor Paul) to live unashamed, confident in God. I couldn't write these words for you if I hadn't been Spirit-restored and enabled to do so through my own cooperation with God's grace. I hope that by way of self-compassion, you may find your own freedom from shame and look at yourself the gracious way Jesus looks at you.

You told me who I am,
whose I am: myself and yours.
Undo, my God, the damage done
to your image in my flesh.
Restore in me the dignity I embodied
before cruelty obstructed
my access to the truth.
Amen.

Saturday of Week 4

Writing Compassion

I am writing to you, little children, because your sins are forgiven on account of his name. I am writing to you, fathers,
because you know him who is from the beginning. I am writing to you, young people, because you have conquered the evil
one. I write to you, children, because you know the Father.
I write to you, fathers, because you know him who is from
the beginning. I write to you, young people, because you are
strong and the word of God abides in you, and you have overcome the evil one.

—1 John 2:12–14

*I took up my pen and wrote your name in my book. I wrote
your story even before you were conceived in the flesh. You are
my dream-words, my poetry lines, my lyrical list of the days
that will comprise your earthly life. I contemplated and composed you, yet I set you free to act as you choose, to imagine
and create, to work and serve, to love and strive and struggle
and thrive. I have provided spacious margins on your story's
pages. Take up your own pen. What will you write?*

At a retreat center on the edge of Saguaro National Park, a dozen or
so adults of various ages and ethnic backgrounds gather to learn the
art of spiritual direction. Outside the windows of the classroom, on
rocky, sunbaked hillsides, giant saguaro cactuses grow by the hundreds, their ribbed, spiney trunks erect, thick and tall as telephone

115

poles. Mature saguaros' upward-bending arms give the impression they're offering a benediction.

The students are Protestant, Roman Catholic, Unitarian, and "Spiritual but Not Religious." They are women and men, clergy and laity, straight and queer, US-born, and, in a few cases, from other countries. They are more, of course, than a summary can say. They are beloved of God and have enrolled in this program to become equipped to help other spiritual seekers live in responsive relationship with God. Over the years that I've taught in the program, I've introduced the students to "Desert Spirituality" and "Writing as a Spiritual Practice," among other topics.

Picture Rocks Road, where the retreat center stands, is named for petroglyphs—animal, human, and abstract symbols that Hohokam people chipped onto the face of large rocks roughly a thousand years ago. Images of hunters, dancers, shamans, and spirals remind present-day visitors that for indigenous inhabitants past and present, Sonoran land and all of life are sacred.

This is a good place for prospective spiritual directors to learn to watch for signs of divine design in their own and others' lives. The retreat center's program is called the Hesychia School of Spiritual Direction. *Hesychia* (pronounced *Heh zuh kEYE uh* or *Heh zuh KEY uh*) is a Greek word meaning stillness, quiet, silence. The Desert Mothers and Fathers of the fourth and fifth centuries, those early Christians who left cities to live contemplative lives in the Nile River Valley, were called hesychasts, so deeply did they value the simplicity and solitude they found in the desert.

They also found that in the desert's silence, the troubles in their minds, from which busy, urban life had formerly distracted them, could not be ignored. Evagrius, the Desert Father I introduced you to earlier this week, called these internal troubles by two names: "thoughts" and "demons." The latter term can be hard for present-day people to appreciate, connoting as it does a supernatural worldview out of step with most contemporary understandings of psychology and spirituality. Yet "wrestling with demons" is a common colloquial expression for grappling with mental and emotional difficulties that also interfere with spiritual life. Intrusive, disruptive thoughts (to use Evagrius' other term) are often connected to depression, anxiety, anger, addiction, and other "demons" with which people of any era may contend.

Paul Gilbert, one of the psychologists I mentioned in yesterday's reflection, recommends writing to counteract destructive thought patterns. In particular, Gilbert suggests writing yourself a letter as a rational, expressive way to direct your thinking away from self-condemnation and toward self-compassion. A helpfully self-compassionate letter may accomplish a number of purposes: express sensitivity to your own distress and needs, show sympathy and loving-kindness toward yourself, process difficult emotions, provide a safe space where distress may become more tolerable, reflect on your dilemmas to help you understand them, refrain from negative judgmentalism, convey self-directed loving-kindness throughout, and articulate your thinking about potentially self-helpful behaviors.[1]

Since the global pandemic, social injustices, and international conflicts of the 2020s erupted, many people's mental health has taken some hard hits. As this fourth week of Lent comes to a close, perhaps you would benefit from writing yourself a compassionate letter. Might you set apart a portion of this very day as a mindful "*hesychia* time" for writing?

Before you begin writing a letter to yourself, look at the passage from John's first New Testament letter at the beginning of this reflection. Take it personally, as though you are (because you are!) among the intended recipients of John's affirming words. You rightly belong to the community of forgiven, strong, and knowing people in whom God's word abides, capable of overcoming demons of destructive thought.

Listen in prayerful silence for God's Spirit speaking in you, then begin to write to yourself as you would write an understanding letter to affirm a dear friend. You could even draw "glyphs" in your letter— simple symbols and signs to express your sense of belonging among the people of God, who holds you and holds all living beings in rock-steady mercy and love.

When they tried to teach me to be somebody else,
I disappointed my instructors and confused myself.
My Creator, my Rock, read over my shoulder
while I write myself a loving-kindness letter.
Lead me to unlearn their lousy lessons.

Disempower demons of self-doubt. Writing
my rights and wrongs, songs and silliness and longings,
may I accept myself
as you, the Author of my life,
accept me with compassion in as-is condition.
Amen.

Week 5

Do Not Condemn

Sabbath Rest Stop

When I was a little kid, an irritated grown-up in my life sometimes hissed the word, "Damnation!" I heard the "nation" part of "damnation" and wondered if it was a terrible country. I knew for sure it was a bad word because I used it once and that same grown-up said, "I have a surprise for you! Close your eyes and open your mouth." Expecting candy, I complied. Suddenly a whole bar of soap, slimy and perfumy, was on my tongue. I spat into the kitchen sink and concluded that the world was an off-kilter place. People meant to protect and teach you could trick and condemn you for imitating them.

Consider the damage this kind of treatment does to a kid. As supposedly responsible grown-ups all too commonly do to children, people older and more powerful than I condemned me early and often. I became wrongly convinced of my unlovability and God's mean-spirited absenteeism. *Condemn*, the word itself, is rooted in *damn*. To condemn a child is to say, "Go to hell."

Hell is no place to live. That's why I've devoted this Lenten journey, and my life, really, to Jesus and his teaching that the kin-dom of God is at hand, here and now. In this very day, this moment, he points the way from damnation to salvation: "Be compassionate," Jesus says, "just as your Father is compassionate. Don't judge, and you won't be judged. Don't condemn, and you won't be condemned. Forgive, and you will be forgiven" (Luke 6:36–37, CEB).

In my work, I listen to people who need a human reminder that God listens nonjudgmentally to them. Sometimes they say damning things about themselves. It's as though long ago they swallowed someone's condemnation and have been spitting up bitter soap ever since. There's nothing cleansing about the damnation that is condemnation. For people who were condemned early and often, punished for behaving only as damnably as they'd been treated, the condemnation stuck, deep in the craw.

Jesus' followers sometimes succumb to the temptation to condemn as they have been condemned. The cycle is difficult to break. A whole culture of condemnation taught them to confuse retribution and redemption. Victims of an off-kilter, vengeful worldview commonly reproduce the condemnation they received. People tend to give what they got, to pay the pain forward. Hurt people hurt people. So goes the emotional logic of mistreatment and damnation. But another kind of logic, of love, is possible.

Jesus' compassionate commandment, *Don't condemn and you won't be condemned*, could be altered to express another truth: *Don't condemn and you won't perpetuate the cycle of condemnation*. Let me break the cycle. Let compassion start with me.

When Jesus, holy disrupter that he was, taught his followers to renounce condemning others, he knew full well they lived, as he lived, in a culture of condemnation. Common thieves could be publicly crucified for their crimes, to say nothing of Jesus himself, an innocent scapegoat whose only offense was to shine a clear, compassionate light on the condemnatory norms of an off-kilter world. Anointed to love this world into a whole new integrity and balance, Jesus urged people to refuse to harm others as they had been harmed, and thereby break the dehumanizing cycle of condemnation. Even while dying, a wrongfully condemned and crucified man, Jesus asked God to forgive his condemners. They didn't understand that they, themselves, were victims. They were perpetuating the damnation they had seen and suffered all their lives. What good would God have done to make it last forever?

The fifth week of Lent begins today. Signs of crucifixion appear on the nearing horizon. The Christian cycle of remembering Jesus' ultimate experience can seem like merely reproducing trauma. Again and again, he sets his face toward Jerusalem. Again and again, the faithful follow, only to stumble once more where their faithfulness bumps up against their capacity for betrayal and denial. The story can't be rewritten, but it can be rethought, reprocessed toward a better purpose than guilt, shame, and punishment.

Approach the threshold between your abilities and your limitations forgivingly. Choose to see yourself as you are, God's beloved work in progress. Notice the condemnatory impulse you may feel toward yourself and other unfinished people. Choose mercy.

So far, this devotional guide to the desert of compassion has encouraged you to let your heart be softened, your hand be extended in loving-kindness, your wakeful endurance of distress become deepened, and your mind be engaged in cultivating loving-kindness. It's a lot to ask. I wouldn't ask it if I didn't know that God is in the desert with you and with anyone who dares to follow Jesus there.

Today, rest guiltlessly. If you can, let this Sabbath be a day of re-creation. The week ahead will bring enough demands. It will also offer you an invitation: to identify the damning traps, the merciless habits of history, collective and personal, that impede people's access to God's recreative compassion. Together, you and I can circumvent a few of those traps, help others avoid them, and even dismantle them with love.

Monday of Week 5

City of Refuge

Joab sent to Tekoa and brought from there a wise woman. He said to her, "Pretend to be a mourner; put on mourning garments, do not anoint yourself with oil, but behave like a woman who has been mourning many days for the dead. Go to the king and speak to him as follows." And Joab put the words into her mouth. . . . "We must all die; we are like water spilled on the ground, which cannot be gathered up. But God will not take away a life; he will devise plans so as not to keep an outcast banished forever from his presence."

—2 Samuel 14:2–3, 14

I devise plans to bring you back. I will gather and welcome you regardless of the path you took that led you from my presence. Come back, my beloved, come home.

Before today, were you familiar with the woman from Tekoa? Like the names of many women mentioned in the Bible, hers is unknown. I call her Takouhy, the name of my Armenian great aunt. It means "queen" or "royalty" and sounds like "Tekoite," the name for a resident of Tekoa.

The Tekoite woman was neither a queen nor a prophet, but according to Second Samuel, she was wise and persuasive. With remarkable confidence, Takouhy addressed King David. She portrayed a grieving widow, told the king an invented tale of family woe, and even theologized to accomplish her rhetorical purpose. She was working for another man, Joab, who wanted David to allow his exiled son, Absalom, to come back home. Joab directed Takouhy's performance for the king, but she made the role her own, acting so convincingly that David finally relented from condemning Absalom. In doing so, as Takouhy had pointed out, David realized God's own plans "not to keep an outcast banished forever."

Sermonizing on the fourteenth chapter of Second Samuel, the renowned nineteenth-century preacher and abolitionist Charles Spurgeon proclaimed the spiritual restoration of people once separated from God: "The ever-blessed God has devised means by which we may be delivered from this state of exile; and the means are very similar to that which was alluded to by the woman of Tekoa. He has set apart Jesus Christ to be to us a City of Refuge and a High Priest."[1]

In the twentieth century, the Brief Statement of Faith affirmed Jesus as the restorer of people pushed to the margins of society:

> Jesus proclaimed the reign of God: preaching good news to the poor and release to the captives, teaching by word and deed and blessing the children, healing the sick and binding up the brokenhearted, eating with outcasts, forgiving sinners, and calling all to repent and believe the gospel.[2]

The recurrent scriptural message is timeless and clear: God liberates exiles and extravagantly welcomes them to return to life among neighbors. Jesus breaks the bonds of captivity and breaks bread with those whom others have condemned.

But I wonder what Second Samuel doesn't say. What motivated the woman I call Takouhy to convince King David to end Absalom's exilic condemnation? Had Joab, her director, given her little choice? Had he paid her handsomely? She seems to have had her own reasons to angle for the freedom of Absalom, who was no innocent. He had contrived to end the life of his brother, Amnon, who, appallingly, had raped their half-sister, Tamar. It's a cast of wounded, wounding, wily characters that people many of the Bible's books. Some behave so condemnably or suffer so profoundly that their stories can still shock readers.

Sometimes it's a shock of recognition. You and I can see ourselves reflected in biblical strugglers and strivers and sense our own need to be freed from condemnation and our own impulse to condemn. Taken as a whole, the Bible can be read as a roadmap to the "city of refuge" where Jesus heals, helps, forgives, and feeds all comers. All comers? You may reasonably ask. Rapists and murderers? All comers. All refugees from the cities of obsession, oppression, violence, and condemnation—externally imposed and internally imprinted on the psyche—can find forgiveness and redemption in God, or nobody can. This is the heart and substance of Takouhy's compelling appeal to King David: "God will not take away a life [but] . . . will devise a plan" to save every life, including that of someone you or I may deem unworthy of salvation.

The Lenten desert leads to Jesus' unjust and brutal condemnation by wounded, wounding people. Jesus' teaching, "Do not condemn" is a compass needle pointing toward another way. Compassion is the path through the desert and the goal of Jesus' followers, including, as the Scriptures witness and the creeds affirm, the captives and the sick, the brokenhearted outcasts, the sinners who languish unforgiven until they are found by the rarest of friends: "God of compassion, in mercy befriend us," wrote hymnist John J. Moment. "Though we are lost, you have sought us and found us."[3]

This world's Amnons and Absaloms are people whose humanity has been horribly misshapen and misled. If I refuse to behold them with compassion, then I must imagine God's love is as conditional as mine, and God's mercy is reserved only for the good who need it least. That's too paltry a theology for me, and, I hope, for you. I stand with Takouhy. Will you join me? Serpentine in her wisdom, dovelike in her honesty, she appeals to the person who has power to condemn, urging: *Do not condemn. Do the braver thing. Relent from punishing, and even more, forgive.*

God of compassion,
Friend of the friendless,
you reach out to me
and in mercy encompass
my life: my wounds
and failings, strengths, wisdom,
foolishness, and wit,
all of it, all of me
you embrace. And why

would you do less
for anybody else? Help me
accept your compassion
and point others toward the city
of your refuge.
Amen.

Tuesday of Week 5

Violence Is Never Redemptive

"I have a hope in God—a hope that they themselves also accept—that there will be a resurrection of both the righteous and the unrighteous. Therefore I do my best always to have a clear conscience toward God and all people."

—Acts 24:15–16

Lay down your arms and lift up your hearts. Raise your hands and lift up your voices. Sing with me this glorious chorus: I will raise them to new life! I will save my people!

I find myself speaking of war. I preach sermons that address military aggression yet proclaim God's saving love. I talk privately with people made heartsick by news of refugees fleeing by the millions for their lives. I don't want to speak of war any more than I want one nation to wage war on another. I have no choice about the latter, so I choose to do the former. I say what I see in Jesus' life, death, and resurrection: God's nonviolent love dismantling death-dealing powers.

How fortunate I am to be free to talk of war without experiencing it. I haven't been forced from my country. I will go to sleep tonight not in a gymnasium-turned-shelter, not on a makeshift mattress, but in my own safe home, in my own soft bed, confident no neighboring nation's army will transgress the borders of this one before dawn.

I listen to others—at times in grave astonishment. People talk of assassinating world leaders whose policies and actions they deplore. Reasonable people, caring, thoughtful, sane, educated, everyday people talk about "taking out" a tyrant, of praying he will die, of giving him a taste of his own poison to render him helpless—alive but unable to speak or move. "This," one troubled clergy colleague of mine intimated, "may be our Bonhoeffer moment." Born in Germany in 1906, Dietrich Bonhoeffer was a Lutheran pastor, theologian, pacifist, and Nazi resistor. His brother-in-law, Hans von Dohnanyi, a highly placed professional in the German Reich, was a clandestine Nazi resistor who plotted with others to assassinate Adolf Hitler. Bonhoeffer's participation in the assassination plot is widely accepted as fact (hence the "Bonhoeffer moment" remark), but some researchers argue that he remained a committed pacifist throughout his life.

Reminiscent of the Apostle Paul, who hoped in God "that there will be a resurrection of both the righteous and the unrighteous," Bonhoeffer believed in a "universal Christian" siblinghood that transcended national identity and difference. He was an ecumenically minded person who visited numerous countries, including the United States. His experience of African American spirituality, especially sacred songs and prophetic preaching, made a profound impression on him.

He was ordained in Berlin in 1931, but within two years, his pastoral ministry became impossibly circumscribed by Nazism and the blasphemous equation of the German Führer with the risen Lord. Bonhoeffer signed the Theological Declaration of Barmen, a Christian confessional statement that repeatedly rejected as false any teaching that subordinated Christ to the state or advanced totalitarianism. Theologian Karl Barth, who drafted the declaration, later chided Bonhoeffer for leaving Germany in 1933 to serve German-speaking churches in London. Barth believed Bonhoeffer had abandoned the people who most needed his ministry. But even Bonhoeffer's friends had not supported his dissident views, which he continued to promote while in London. Notably, he said of his departure for that city that "it was about time to go for a while into the desert."[1]

Rarely has London, a crowded, often rainy metropolis, been described as a desert. The desert comment meant that like Jesus, Spirit-led into the Judean wilderness, Bonhoeffer stepped away from the political fray to get down to the essence of his faith, identity, convictions, and calling. He had refused to lead a church in Berlin (where he had been offered a pastoral position) that would serve only "Aryan" people. His controversial views—righteous though they were—meant that his closest associates deserted him. In London, he sought solace in the spiritual desert of prayer and in the humble work of caring for souls.

Bonhoeffer's best-known book, *The Cost of Discipleship*, was published in 1937, two years after he returned to Berlin from London. In it, he wrote knowingly,

> The messengers of Jesus will be hated to the end of time. They will be blamed for all the divisions which rend cities and homes. Jesus and his disciples will be condemned on all sides for undermining family life, and for leading the nation astray; they will be called crazy fanatics and disturbers of the peace. The disciples will be sorely tempted to desert their Lord. But the end is also near, and they must hold on and persevere until it comes. Only he will be blessed who remains loyal to Jesus and his word until the end.[2]

"This is the end—for me, the beginning of life," were Bonhoeffer's parting words to another inmate in the Nazi concentration camp where he was hanged in 1945. This was the real "Bonhoeffer moment." A person of brilliance and peace, having persevered in costly loyalty to Jesus, accepted that the evil he'd opposed would destroy him as it had destroyed millions of other human beings. On his way to the gallows, he proclaimed resurrection hope.

Bonhoeffer's moment of fearless faith exposes the fantasies of wannabe tyrant-assassins for what they are: cheap reproductions of evil in the guise of the good. Don't be fooled by armchair talk of schemes to take out tyrants. Jesus, wounded-yet-risen, will tell you violence is never redemptive. Love and only love will ever overcome evil.

Lord of life, Risen One,
let my days proclaim the love
by which you save this warring world
from those hellbent on its destruction.
Amen.

Wednesday of Week 5

What Mercy Means

"But if you had known what this means, 'I desire mercy and
not sacrifice,' you would not have condemned the guiltless."
—Matthew 12:7

My love for you, crystalline and old as earth, endures. Pres-
sure, darkness, fire, burial, and time do not destroy but refine
my love for you, lasting as a diamond, twice as shining.

I'm going to ask you to do a hard thing. Think back to something
you said, a remark so barbed it tore your lip as you spoke, which you
would unsay if you could. Or remember something unkind you did
that you wish you could undo.

Pause. Remember.

When a person of conscience lashes out at someone else, not only
is the targeted person hurt. For the perpetrator, there's the added kick-
back pain of shock and shame. You may not recall the hurtful words
you said so much as the aftermath, when you saw yourself as not only
capable of causing harm, but guilty of doing so. This is hard stuff to
face. Yet I encourage you to bring your regrettable remark or action
to mind because there may yet be light to cull from that shadow.

Pause. Pray. Let the shadow come into view.

"Shadow" is a term that psychologist Carl Jung coined to describe
aspects of ourselves that human beings try to hide or disown. Coming
to know yourself, including the parts you may be loath to acknowledge,
is crucial to mental health and wholeness. An unacknowledged shadow

131

doesn't disappear. Disowning the shadow takes emotional energy that could be better spent developing courageous self-awareness.

To know the fullest possible truth of who you are—shadow and light alike—is to know the Creator in whose image you were made, in whom "darkness is as light" (Ps. 139:12). As well as destructive potential, the shadow can contain disowned goodness. You may possess constructive capacities and gifts of which you're largely unaware. The shadow holds energy that, freed-up and brought to light, can mobilize you to live with greater daring and creativity.

The Pharisees in the Gospels serve as shadow figures, judgmental, holier-than-thou know-it-alls who never break a law or think an impure thought. They represent humankind cut off from its totality, throwing shade on others instead of owning their flawed complexity. In reality, Pharisees were multidimensional people who chose to live as religious separatists. By separating themselves from neighbors and condemning them as unlawful or unclean, they truncated their own humanity and failed to understand crucial aspects of the Scriptures and the God they professed to follow.

Literarily speaking, the Gospel writers used Pharisees as foils whose sanctimonious cruelty made Jesus' wise loving-kindness look all the more luminous. The Gospels' portrayals make the Pharisees easy for readers to condemn. That's a hazard for people who want to cultivate compassion for everyone and not only for lovable people who deserve it.

Jesus wanted people to cultivate in themselves the compassion for others that he demonstrated was possible with God's help. Ironically, the Gospels tend not to depict Jesus acting with compassion toward the Pharisees, but rather exposing their condemnatory ways as unholy. The Pharisees' spiritual and moral arrogance prompted Jesus to critique merciless religion and show mercy to its victims— the hungry, the poor, and people deemed impure. Jesus illuminated the path of God, who desires not rule-bound religion that condemns people in need, but faithful disciples who care without judgmentalism for their neighbors.

Jesus taught people to practice a love for which there is no adequate English word. The Hebrew word *chesed* (pronounced KHEH-sed, with two short *e*'s), commonly translated as *mercy* or *loving-kindness*, signifies spiritual commitment and practical compassion. To the rhetorical question, "Do you want to be right or do you want to be kind?" *chesed* is the answer. *Chesed* calls pharisaism's bluff.

"Be kind," the saying goes, "for everyone you know is fighting a hard battle." Often misattributed to Plato or Philo of Alexandria, the saying probably originated with a nineteenth-century Briton named John Watson who pastored Scottish churches and authored numerous books. One of these contains this sensitive call for compassion: "This man beside us also has a hard fight with an unfavouring world, with strong temptations, with doubts and fears, with wounds of the past which have skinned over, but which smart when they are touched."[1]

At the beginning of this reflection, I asked you to bring to mind a still-smarting wound of the past and do an even harder thing: face the fact that you caused it. Be kind to yourself as you fight the urge not to know the shadow. Let that disavowed, half-forgotten wound—the one you caused and the secondary one you bear from having hurt another person—be touched by the light of your awareness and the *chesed* God is calling you to cultivate.

Chesed is another name for grace, the forgiving, merciful, and liberating love of God that dismantles condemnation and dignifies the person who accepts it. You—regrets and all—are bathed in the light of God's *chesed*-grace. Realize this and the shadow will shrink, no longer overburdened with condemnable contents. See yourself as Jesus sees you, freed from pharisaical scorn to be who you are, a multidimensional human being, entirely beloved. It's this acceptance—God's of you and yours of *chesed*—that enables you to refrain from condemning others and treat with compassion anyone who "has a hard fight with an unfavoring world."

If I had known the impact of my words
before I said them,
I would have eaten them
as disciples in the fields ate grain they plucked on the Sabbath.
I would have ground down those words in my mouth,
tasted their truth, taken it in, let it be part of me,
let myself be as you let me be:
imperfect, forgiven, and given another opportunity
to learn the meaning of your mercy.
Amen.

Thursday of Week 5

Long-Haul Healing

> What should I say to you? Should I commend you? In this
> matter I do not commend you!
>
> —1 Corinthians 11:22b

The feet of the one who stepped on yours, I wash. I pour heal-
ing ointment on your crushed skin. I am love without con-
dition. Without contempt for anyone, I condemn sin and I
forgive sinners. I commend you and your enemy equally to
my salvation.

The desert that Lent beckons you to cross runs long. Lent's long history stretches back to the fourth century. In 325 CE, the First Council
of Nicaea convened on what is now the western coast of the Republic of Türkiye. Bishops in attendance, having come to consensus on
Christ's identity and divinity, wrote the Nicene Creed, which remains
a cornerstone of Christian orthodoxy. Soon, Lent became established
as a forty-day (forty-six, if you count Sundays) sacred season of fasting, repentance, baptismal preparation for new Christian converts,
and Easter preparation for all the faithful.

People's Lenten observances sometimes short-circuit because of
flagging stamina or demanding distractions. But there are no shortcuts through the season. Lent's length never varies (remember, the
word "Lent" is linked with "lengthen").

There's time enough in Lent to get a little lost and still find your
way back to the path through the desert that you set out intending to

follow to the end. If you've come to this day late in Lent's fifth week having skipped over or wandered away from compassionate intentions you set in week one, trust that God never lost sight of you and never will. Welcome back. Press on. Easter isn't here yet. Lent stretches on. While writing these devotions for the Lenten journey through the desert of compassion, I've experienced a few of my own "are we there yet?" moments. I'm not immune to the temptation to skip ahead and get to the good part in a hurry.

"Spiritual bypassing" is a term that writer John Welwood coined to describe the use of spiritual belief and practice to avoid turmoil and pain and expedite inner peace. Think of Frank Costanza played by Jerry Stiller on *Seinfeld*. On the advice of an audio self-help recording, every time he feels angry, Frank yells "Serenity now!" It's funny but it's futile. Hustled forgiveness or suppressive prayer may seem to work in the short run, but will produce counterfeit, short-lived serenity, at best. The peace that surpasses understanding can't be achieved by spiritual bypassing. It's a gift of grace that comes in time, through an honest, transformative relationship with yourself and God (Phil. 4:6–7).

I once consulted a counselor about my lingering pain over a person who had betrayed me. The counselor adopted a gruff sports coachlike demeanor, goading and cajoling me to say over and over, "I forgive them! I forgive them!" It wasn't funny like Frank Costanza's "serenity now!" but I assure you, it was every bit as ridiculous. Yes, forgiving does involve making a conscious choice. And yes, disrupting negative mental patterns with positive messages can constructively redirect thoughts. But repeatedly mouthing words you don't mean and self-badgering in the guise of spiritual practice is fruitless and hazardous to your health. Don't do it. You'd be better off admitting to yourself, to God, and to a trustworthy third party, "The truth is, I don't forgive them. Yet." Let the truth set you free from the lie that *it's all good.* Honesty lays the groundwork for genuine transformation.

Spiritual bypassing often amounts to saying something was OK that wasn't OK. Many people, especially women, have been conditioned emotionally and culturally to allow others to violate their boundaries. Their internalized false directives say, *Whatever you do, avoid confrontation and conflict. Be nice. Don't make it a big deal. Pray it away. Forgive and forget. Bless their hearts.* Spiritual bypassing may also entail (as it did for me with the misguided counselor) forcing or faking freedom from unresolved feelings that need to be felt before any healing can happen.

If you want to make the journey to genuine redemption, pack water, wear a wide-brimmed hat and tough-soled shoes, and keep on trekking, deeper into the desert. If you haven't yet reckoned with the loss, the betrayal, the pain that comprises your desert's toughest stretch, maybe it's time to face it and work through it. Maybe you're strong enough now to quit skirting those spiny agaves they call shin daggers. Maybe you're prepared now to harvest the hooked fruits of the devil's claw plant, to get to the goodness hidden behind the prohibitive guise. With prayerful care and a compassionate companion, you can venture into the thick of your life story.

The prickly people you've encountered on your journey may look downright condemnable. Like Paul, who in this reflection's opening verse frankly calls out the Corinthians' exclusionary practices, you may find it necessary to condemn behaviors you cannot commend. Notice I say "condemn *behaviors*." This is different from condemning *behavers*. It's possible to honor people's essential dignity while constructively condemning their hurtful actions. This often-thorny differentiation of the behaver from the behavior is not to be undertaken carelessly. But it's crucial to life in Christ, who teaches his followers to love their enemies. Loving people does not mean condoning their wrongful acts. Love does not consist of pretending those who hurt you didn't. At its toughest, love includes acknowledging, resisting, and renouncing misconduct.

For the sake of your wholeness, might you now face full-on some scrapes and deeper injuries you sustained getting to this place where you find yourself today? Telling the truth of what you've been through can lead you to the desert's oasis—the interior rest area where God's compassion awaits you. There, wounds can become scars—injuries not forgotten but graciously, gradually healed.

If I hold my enemies in contempt,
Lord, in your greater mercy than mine,
protect them, correct me,
and heal us all from the cyclical

sickness of sin inflicted
and retaliated. Break
the cycle before we break
each other.
Amen.

Friday of Week 5

Sore Need and Sacred Affirmation

To err is human.

> Indeed, God did not send the Son into the world to condemn the world, but in order that the world might be saved through him.
>
> —John 3:17

My saving love cannot be calculated, but it can be dreamed. See it in your mind: water bubbling up in a dry land, freshening cracked earth, soaking roots of tall trees. Bask in their shade. Rest your back against a trunk. Rest and know I hold you dear, just as you are.

For some of us, it's a short jump from hearing Jesus' teachings to feeling ashamed for falling short in our efforts to carry them out. Jesus says, "Love your enemies." Many of us treat our enemies better than we treat ourselves. We put ourselves down; we take on blame that isn't ours to bear; we become good at treating ourselves badly, as though we're unworthy of the same love Jesus calls us to give even to those who do us harm.

Some of us came of age being told we were somehow deficient. We believed it, and our religion may have reinforced the message. Some flavors of Christianity place a heavy stress on human sinfulness, zeroing in on all the ways we fail to love our enemies and fail to do good, expecting nothing in return.

Now, it is important that we assess ourselves honestly and acknowledge the ways we need to grow in grace, because only then can we open ourselves to being transformed by God's freely offered mercy and wisdom. This is why, in worship services, we pray prayers of confession about our brokenness and our need for forgiveness. The Prayer of Confession and the Words of Assurance remind us: we are works in progress; we get some things wrong; but God's amazing grace heals us and sets us on a right path.

Isn't it also important to notice the ways that—God helping us—we get it right? We, who inherited a sin-concerned faith tradition, and those who were personally told, early and often, that they didn't measure up, would do well to celebrate with God and with each other the sins we don't commit, the ways we do rise to difficult occasions, the times we treat other people as we want to be treated, and the times we treat ourselves with respect and compassion.

I once preached a sermon with this message, and one congregant, smiling and wide-eyed, told me, "I've never heard that in church before!" It saddens but doesn't surprise me that an affirming, anti-condemnatory sermon strikes some listeners as rare. Throughout my pastoral career, I've encountered plenty of people who were recovering (or trying to recover) from condemnatory religion. Too many times, they were called "sinners" and their humanity was reduced to fallenness and depravity.

Those who leave Christianity often say they do so to disaffiliate from a tradition they perceive as shaming and unreflective of God's love. Citing cultural and religious trends tracked by the Barna Group, one publication for church leaders includes this claim: "Across the nation, a large percentage of unchurched people have negative views of the church, thinking that local churches are judgmental, hypocritical, irrelevant, disconnected from real issues in the community, and known more for what they are against."[1]

The public perception of Christianity as a condemnatory faith may be influenced not only by bad messages received at church, but also by the human brain's reactivity to perceived threats. "Negativity bias" is the name neuroscientists and psychologists have given to the documented human tendency to respond to negative events more forcefully than to positive events of equal intensity. Theoretically, the negativity bias enhanced human evolution. The human brain evolved such that threats loom large, alerting us to danger and prompting us to protect our safety and that of our young. From an evolutionary perspective, the negativity bias was more helpful to our survival than accentuating the positive would have been.

If you ever wonder why you seem to focus disproportionately on the one lousy aspect of an otherwise lovely day, it's because you're human and you have an evolutionary hangover. The fittest members of our species survived in part by accentuating the negative—the risk of a lion attack, for example. But trouble can arise when the primal, survival mechanism overrides the brain's subtler capacities to reason, reflect, discern, and relate positively with others. For example, when a fire-and-brimstone preacher threatens listeners with damnation, the negatively biased brain may conclude that the church—not just a single congregation with a scary leader, but the whole Christian community—is a dangerous fellowship that serves a condemnatory God. *Run for your life*, says the brain. And the many congregations whose preachers proclaim God's compassion, welcome, inclusion, and justice, whose members embody these values beautifully, become perceptually lumped in with the dreaded church that loves to hate sinners and condemn unbelievers.

Maybe you know people, as I do, who suffer from loneliness and soul-thirst because they've been religiously wounded. They're stuck in a spiritual desert, never having found their way to the wellspring of compassion that is an accepting, loving spiritual community. Paul Gilbert, the founder of Compassion Focused Therapy, whose work I mentioned last week, notes that "many psychological difficulties are rooted in social relational problems"[2] such as people's lack of affirmation and compassion *from* others, their underdeveloped care and concern *for* others, and their inability to see themselves as worthy, beloved beings.

A faithful Christian community addresses these kinds of difficulties by celebrating and sharing divine love, teaching neighbor-love, and cultivating healthy self-love among its members. Despite widespread negative perceptions of the church, wherever the Christian community perseveres in caring as Jesus cares, people do learn, deep-down, that God is all-compassion, and spiritually, they thrive.

Wash away the stain
condemnation left on the brain.
Rinse your beloved
in waters of blessing, O God,
in cleansing rains of renewal.
Amen.

Saturday of Week 5

The Uncondemned Woman

> Jesus straightened up and said to her, "Woman, where are they? Has no one condemned you?" She said, "No one, sir." And Jesus said, "Neither do I condemn you. Go your way, and from now on do not sin again."
>
> —John 8:10–11

I am the Stonebreaker, Lifesaver, Revealer of thugs' guilt and impotence, Dismantler of manipulators' sinister schemes, Hearer of screams, of silences, of hearts' fearful thundering. I am the Name fingered into the earth, the Finger pointed back at cruel judges, the Writer of the new law, the Freer of terrorized women, the Healer of their ruined flesh and broken minds. I am the Restorer of humankind and I honor you as you are.

She's commonly referred to as "the woman caught in adultery." The Gospel writer John portrays her accusers as claiming to have caught her in the act. Did she have a choice? Did she exert agency and personal power in the adulterous liaison? Was she guilty, or was she victimized, forced into sex, then bullied and shamed by a gang of men? Had they raped her? And was it really John who wrote her story? Provocative questions, both about textual legitimacy and the untold aspects of the woman's experience, surround this Scripture.

One of the Bible's best-known anti-condemnatory verses, spoken by Jesus, functions as the story's moral fulcrum: "Let anyone who is without sin be the first to throw a stone at her" (John 8:7b). On this rhetorical *gotcha*, the narrative pivots. For a second time, Jesus bends down to write a message with his finger in the sandy soil. The woman's accusers skulk away. Left alone, Jesus and the woman exchange words. He saves her not only from physical harm but also from the spiritual consequences of breaking the commandment against adultery. The story reinforces Jesus' image as a holy man of unequaled compassion, especially for vulnerable, outcast people.

Yet some argue that the story of the uncondemned woman shouldn't even be included in the Bible. In the oldest, most authoritative manuscripts of John's Gospel, the story doesn't appear. It's written in a style atypical of John. Interpreters are divided on the question of whether the incident really happened during Jesus' ministry. Trying to resolve such puzzles definitively is like trying to decipher the messages Jesus wrote with his finger on the ground.

Whatever its backstory may be, the *Pericope Adulterae* (as John 8:1–11 is known by scholars) bears the fingerprint of the loving Liberator depicted in many other Gospel stories. For this reason, most Bible readers remain untroubled by (if they're even aware of) the story's dubious authenticity; many would be troubled by its removal from John's account.

What is the nature of your relationship with Scripture? Were you raised on the Bible? Did you ingest its wisdom with your first bites of solid food? Have you read it for spiritual wisdom and guidance ever since? Did you, like me, begin to read the Bible in adulthood? Do you feel largely unfamiliar with the book?

A now-deceased congregant once told me she wanted to attend Bible study but never would because her basic scriptural ignorance embarrassed her. She was probably telling me the truth, but it occurs to me she may not have wanted to go to Bible study yet felt compelled to make up an excuse. She was a complicated woman with tattooed eyebrows and wicked sense of humor. She may not have known the Bible well, but she knew the love of Jesus and could put it into practice with dovelike gentleness and serpentine smarts. When her husband (also now deceased) tried to bully me into pastoring the church according to his dictates, it was she who got him to back down.

If the story of the uncondemned woman is to be believed (and for the record, I believe it), Jesus used nonviolence and wit instead of aggression and accusation to get religious bullies—armed and ready to stone her to death—to back down. The capital-punitive premise of the *Pericope Adulterae* is archaic and obscene, as Jesus, himself, clearly saw. But this doesn't make the story irrelevant to our own age. Not only is Jesus' takedown of judgmental hypocrites evergreen, but his anti-misogyny still speaks to this world. Consider this excerpt of a Human Rights Watch report on present-day violence against women:

> Honor crimes are acts of violence, usually murder, committed by male family members against female family members who are perceived to have brought dishonor upon the family. . . . A woman can be targeted by her family for a variety of reasons including, refusing to enter into an arranged marriage, being the victim of a sexual assault, seeking a divorce—even from an abusive husband— or committing adultery.[1]

"What most Americans just don't get," argues women's rights activist Ayaan Hirsi Ali, "is that such horrors happen here in the United States of America—and not just in faraway countries like Afghanistan or Somalia."[2] Hirsi Ali, herself a Somalia-born survivor of female genital mutilation, emigrated to Holland in early adulthood and was elected to the Dutch Parliament at age thirty-three. She later became a U.S. citizen. Her outspoken views both draw praise and provoke criticism (some accuse her of islamophobia). She is a polarizing prophet. Nevertheless, the AHA foundation she established has inarguably helped protect girls and women from female genital mutilation, forced marriage, child marriage, and honor violence. Hirsi Ali would likely dismiss any comparison of her work to that of Jesus, but she does share with him a fierce advocacy for abused or potentially abused women, a cause that surely bears the fingerprints of a just and compassionate God.

Strengthen us, Advocate,
Champion of the violated,
to build with defeated oppressors' dropped stones
a refuge in the world where women and girls

may gather and reclaim their bodies, their rights,
their dignity and freedom in your sight.
Wherever your daughters have been
dishonored, murdered, disappeared,
Ruach, *Righteous Wind, blow in.*
Inspire reparations, revolutions.
Amen.

Holy Week

Do This and You Will Live

Palm Sunday Rest Stop

When I read the Gospels, I envision desert places where Jesus walked and taught. I hear braying, squawking beasts and birds and the human din of broadly sunlit, dusty village scenes. Jesus' many neighbors clamor to get to him. Some want a measure of his healing ministrations for themselves or ailing members of their households. Others want Jesus' answers to their spiritual and moral dilemmas. Still others, especially religious leaders, scholars, scribes, and lawyers, want to examine Jesus. Some try to trip him up so they can call him to account for allegedly misleading listeners and causing grave offense to God.

Jesus was a faithful Jewish spiritual teacher, yet fresh and innovative, too, in his interpretations of religious law and in the stories he told. Jesus' parables are lively, relatable narratives that draw people into God's kin-dom, in which, often for the first times in their lives, they experience such compassion that they become able to treat others likewise. Jesus' loving commitment to God and his neighbors was unflagging, unimpeachable. He was the consummate human being, authentically divine.

Jesus' lifetime overlapped with that of the revered sage and scholar, Hillel the Elder, who was instrumental in establishing rabbinic Judaism. Another teacher of this monumental period was Rabbi Tarfon. His teachings appear in the *Pirkei Avot* or *Chapters of the Fathers*, an ancient anthology of rabbinic sayings still widely studied today. Here's an example: "It is not your duty to finish the work, but neither are you free to neglect it."

Does that statement feel familiar to you? It's become part of an encouraging, viral internet meme derived from the contemporary work of Rabbi Rami Shapiro, who draws on the teachings of his forebears. In *Wisdom of the Sages: A Modern Reading of Pirke Avot,* Shapiro combines his own words with those of the biblical prophet Micah (6:8) and Rabbi Tarfon: "Do not be daunted by the enormity of the world's grief. Do justly now, love mercy now, walk humbly now. You are not obligated to complete the work, but neither are you free to abandon it."

This pithy teaching reminds me of Rabbi Hillel's answer to the student who, frustrated with the complexity of the Torah's 613 commandments, challenged his teacher to summarize the five books of Moses while standing on one foot: "That which is despicable to you, do not do to your fellow. This is the whole Torah, and the rest is commentary. Go and learn it."[1]

When a lawyer interrogated Jesus about eternal life and love of neighbor, Jesus answered with a short story. The parable of the Good Samaritan portrays an ordinary traveler who, regardless of ethnic identity, cares for his injured neighbor and provides for his lodging (Luke 10:25–37). "Go and do the same," concludes Rabbi Jesus, and the point cannot be missed: Do justly now, love mercy now, walk humbly now with anyone in need of compassion, and you will walk eternally with God, even now.

The traditional Lenten practices of fasting, prayer, and giving to help impoverished people have always been intended to ground Christians' spiritual lives in practical loving-kindness toward neighbors. When you act to alleviate a neighbor's suffering without presuming to prejudge their worthiness of care, you do your part to realize God's beloved community. It's a wide, welcoming circle of mercy, embodied not in some faraway eternity but right where you are with whoever shows up. Compassion blurs the borderlines between earth and heaven, self and neighbor, giver and receiver, holiness and humanity. Salvation is at hand.

If you can, devote a portion of this Sabbath day to prayer with others. Fast from consuming the kind of content that too often winds up consuming you, leaving you with less love to spare than you had when you first dug in or logged on. Let God's compassion come to you in whatever form you find it, whether by worshiping with others in a Palm Sunday celebration at church, by listening to music that moves your body and spirit, by making love with your partner, or by preparing and sharing a meal with your people. You name it; if it's lifegiving for all concerned, who are weary and aching to put their heavy burdens down, it's compassion, tantamount to a sacrament.

Starting tomorrow and throughout the reflections in this Holy Week, you and I will consider compassion as practical action that redresses neighbors' suffering. Today, may you rest well, love well, and play well, assured that God's love surrounds you and everyone.

Monday of Holy Week

Thread of Creativity

Now in Joppa there was a disciple whose name was Tabitha, which in Greek is Dorcas. She was devoted to good works and acts of charity. . . . All the widows stood . . . weeping and showing tunics and other clothing that Dorcas had made while she was with them.

—Acts 9:36, 39b

A certain woman named Lydia, a worshiper of God, was listening to us; she was from the city of Thyatira and a dealer in purple cloth. The Lord opened her heart to listen eagerly to what was said by Paul. When she and her household were baptized, she urged us, saying, "If you have judged me to be faithful to the Lord, come and stay at my home." And she prevailed upon us.

—Acts 16:14–15

Desiccated mollusks' reeking glandular dyes make weaker vendors cry. But I have made her of strong stuff. She undertakes her labor for my sake, dyeing bolts of flax and silks Tyrian purple, fit for royalty. Seamlessly, she interweaves her garment business with my mission of clothing the naked in beauty. When they are dignified, I am glorified.

My mother's toothy pinking shears munched through garment fabric pinned to tissue paper patterns. Soon, from her sewing room would

150

come the intermittent whir of her machine. She controlled its motor with a pedal underfoot, deftly guiding fabric with her hands. She was a textile organist who made her Singer sing, a motorist who navigated woven yards with silken thread. She clothed her family, all five of us, and if that weren't enough, she upholstered couches, curtained windows. She crafted my wedding dress—unique in all the world—from cobalt blue charmeuse overlaid with creamy lace. In her seventies, she turned to cross stitch, producing miniature replicas of Navajo rugs. But the decades were unkind to her hands and eyes, so in her eighties, she returned to simple knitting, a skill she'd learned at her grandmother's knee before her mother taught her to sew.

I never learned to sew from my mother, though for a stint, she taught sewing basics to others. If I'm crafty, it's with words. But I appreciate the needlecrafts and those who have the patience and persistence to fabricate attire, piece together quilts, crochet coverlets. I once sat through a community theater performance the highlight of which was getting to admire the costume straitjacket a friend of mine had handsewn for free.

Sewing can be a form of *tikkun olam* (Hebrew for "world repair") that helps to mend a torn community. Several sewing members of my congregation participate in Little Dresses for Africa (LDFA). Since its inception in 2008, worldwide LDFA volunteers have fashioned and distributed millions of dresses for girls and "britches for boys" in Malawi, Mozambique, and Zambia, where extreme poverty and social inequity mean that children, many of them parentless, struggle for basic survival. LDFA's Dignity program provides washable pads and underpants that enable menstruating girls to attend school. I love the photos of congregants grinning as they display Little Dresses they've made. Their faces beam with evident pleasure at having crafted, in the words of Teresa of Calcutta, "something beautiful for God." Perhaps the most important aspect of LDFA's work has been the building of two sewing centers in Malawi, including one in a refugee center, where women produce marketable goods and learn financial management skills.

Little Dresses' predecessor in my congregation was Prayers & Squares, an interfaith quilting ministry with hundreds of chapters throughout the U.S. Sewn into each quilt are sturdy threads that congregants tie into a knot while praying for the intended recipient. When

Susan, my mother-in-law of blessed memory, was diagnosed with cancer, she received a Prayers & Squares quilt of remarkable beauty. As intended, it reminded her that she was covered in prayer.

When individual needs and abilities changed in my church, Blessing Blankets emerged as an alternative to Prayers & Squares, thanks to the swift handiwork of one woman whose mission is to bring tangible comfort to anyone who needs it. She insists that each Blessing Blanket given is a gift not from her, but from our whole community of faith. We concur. Where one among us knits, all are linked in love.

I highlight these local and global textile ministries (of which many more examples exist, probably including some in your own community) because in most cases, women are the artisans and their efforts often go unsung. For example, in the U.S.-Mexico borderlands where I live, vital faith-based programs (and the men who historically have led them) that challenge inhumane immigration practices and provide humanitarian aid to migrants, garner vastly more notice than the work of women prayerfully stitching the frayed world back together. Rarely do headlines announce the single industrious knitter who turns a skein of yarn into an afghan for someone to whom her only connection is her calling to alleviate suffering wherever it may occur.

To alleviate suffering is the culminating purpose of your Lenten journey through the desert of compassion. When you offer compassion that goes largely unnoticed, you fulfill a teaching of Jesus commonly proclaimed at Lent's beginning, on Ash Wednesday: "But when you give alms, do not let your left hand know what your right hand is doing, so that your alms may be done in secret; and your Father who sees in secret will reward you" (Matt. 6:3–4).

Jesus respects people's need to find their devotional efforts rewarding. So reap your reward. "Selflessness" is neither a word in Jesus' vocabulary nor a prerequisite to your effective compassionate action. Be devotedly yourself in the spirit of the psalmist who celebrates God the Divine Knitter: "you knit me together in my mother's womb. I praise you, for I am fearfully and wonderfully made" (Ps. 139:13b–14a). Follow the thread of creativity woven into your life and you will contribute sturdy stitches to God's ongoing mending of the unraveled world.

Maker, beribbon with your mercy
my artistry,
so any hurting soul who sees it
may recognize it's really yours
and know the world
will be saved by beauty.[1]
Amen.

Tuesday of Holy Week

Sand and Gold

"And to the angel of the church in Smyrna write: These are the words of the first and the last, who was dead and came to life: . . . . Let anyone who has an ear listen to what the Spirit is saying to the churches. Whoever conquers will not be harmed by the second death."

—Revelation 2:8, 11

All obituaries come to the same grave conclusion. But if you listen for my Spirit speaking to the living, you will hear a new story: One who once was dead has come to life to offer resurrection—life more divinely defiant of death than you knew humankind could live.

Some fifteen years ago, friends of mine, Middle Eastern, Arabic-speaking Christians, found refuge in the United States. Life here isn't easy for them, but they need no longer practice their religion underground or run for their lives from terrorists. For the first time since then, they're preparing to visit the homeland from which violent extremists forced them to flee. Recently they introduced me to a compatriot of theirs who'd gone back to visit their shared country of origin and then returned unharmed. "He's a survivor!" they exulted. And we all laughed—at death.

My Armenian grandfather, Puzant Tarpinian, was a survivor. Before emigrating to Chicago in the 1910s, he grew up in Smyrna (currently

154

called Izmir), an Aegean seaport city on the westernmost edge of what is now officially the Republic of Türkiye. Smyrna was home to one of the seven churches of Revelation named in the New Testament's ultimate, apocalyptic book. Sometime around 1915, Puzant's brother Caspar, my great uncle, died among the estimated one-and-a-half million Armenians systematically exterminated by Turkish nationalists in the Ottoman Empire. To this day, despite international recognition of the Armenian Genocide, Turkish officials deny their nation's historic responsibility for the ethnic annihilation program that also targeted other groups, including Greeks and Syrians. April 24 is Armenian Genocide Remembrance Day. Might you observe it this year by learning about past mass atrocities and global efforts to prevent their future repetition? Bear this in mind: the Third Reich modeled its human extermination policies on the "success" of the Armenian Genocide. Adolf Hitler admired the efficiency with which many Armenians had been forcibly marched into the Syrian desert, where firing squads shot them and buried their bodies in mass graves that they had made the victims dig as their final, earthly act. In "Lord, to You Our People Cry," written for the solemn centenary of the Armenian Genocide, hymnist David Gambrell lyrically recalled this terrible history:

> Lord, to you our people cry; heavy hearts and spirits sigh.
> See what evil we have known, forced upon our flesh and bone:
> Driven from our native land, swept away like desert sand.[1]

I remember my first encounter with the desert, in the American Southwest. The sight of the broad, brilliant landscape stretching toward what appeared to be the far edge of the world shocked me with its strange familiarity. *You have been this way before*, the terrain seemed to say, though I had never previously visited the place. As I was rushing through it in a speeding car, the desert rushed into my consciousness, leveling the decades and denials that had stood between my ancestry and me. It didn't and it doesn't make rational sense, but I was granted a glimpse of the world through which my forebears had passed. I saw the graves of my great uncle and his disappeared generation turned to gold. I had somehow come from there and was destined to return there, eventually to dwell there. The recognition was mutual: I saw the desert and the desert saw me. This had more to do with divine compassion than with facts of geography or genealogy. The desert, as ancient monastics could tell you, is a place of confrontation that summons some people, tests their souls, contours them with the love of God, and reveals them to be insignificant as dust yet precious as gold.

Are you surprised I experienced this vision while traveling through land long and reverently inhabited by indigenous people? I'm not. In what came to be the United States, European colonists once inflicted on Native Americans the same death-dealing tactics Turkish nationalists later deployed against Armenians: religious persecution, death marches, and slaughter. Wherever people crucify people, evil is at work. But Easter Sunday—thank God it's coming soon—will insist that goodness overcomes evil, that resurrection brings about life that can't be taken and reveals truth that can't be covered up. Despite the continuing oppression of indigenous communities in North America, native people persevere with dignity. That's resurrection. Despite their own generational trauma, Armenian communities persist in diaspora. Their lives shine as resurrection signs. God renders gold from desert sand.

My Middle Eastern friends who'll soon make their risky pilgrimage back to the homeland they were forced to desert have been summoned, it seems, to undertake the journey. Practical reasons compel them, involving real estate and a relative's fiancé. Marriages, families, and houses incarnate the human heart's calling to press on defiantly, to live and thrive and rise and love despite the powers that would wipe whole peoples off the planet if they could. The powers do their diabolical damage to be sure, but always, finally, they fail. I'm living proof. I'm descended from a genocide survivor and I'm a Christian, a resurrection woman. I trace my lineage to Smyrna, the city whose church received holy guidance and an everlasting promise from Christ: "Be faithful until death, and I will give you the crown of life" (Rev. 2:10b).

God of memory and presence, you do not desert your people.
When, like Jesus in agony, we feel forsaken, you take on our
   suffering
and let it break your heart.
You let humankind exercise our freedoms as we will—foolishly
or wisely, cruelly or kindly,

but never do you leave us to our own death-dealing ways.
From the very dust in which the meek lie crushed,
you arise and raise us. God of all,
all things fall to you, who lift the crucified to life.
Amen.

Wednesday of Holy Week

Compassion in a Food Desert

> "If only we had meat to eat! We remember the fish we used to
> eat in Egypt for nothing, the cucumbers, the melons, the leeks,
> the onions, and the garlic; but now our strength is dried up."
> —Numbers 11:4b–6a

*When overfed hoarders hog the manna I intend for hungry
people, my anger burns, but not against the poor.*

My friend Shirin McArthur lives in a rapidly developing suburban
neighborhood near Tucson. But, she writes, "we have to drive a dozen
miles to shop in a 'full-service grocery store' rather than a convenience
market. This . . . is usually considered a problem in older urban areas,
not fast-growing suburban neighborhoods, but it seems these [food]
deserts come in all shapes and sizes."[1]

The term "food desert" emerged in the mid-1990s to describe
impoverished geographic areas where people lack access to fresh,
healthy, and affordable food. In urban food deserts rife with fast food
restaurants, people commonly wash down heaps of cheap burgers and
fries with corn syrup-saturated soft drinks. Obesity and its attendant
public health hazards, especially diabetes, afflict at a higher rate people living in food deserts than those who live within a mile of a super-
market and have access to a vehicle.

However, some researchers conclude that even when farmers' mar-
kets and large grocery stores come to poor neighborhoods, residents

158

generally don't change their junk food habits, so the high rates of obesity and diabetes persist.[2] The problem, suggests food historian James McWilliams, goes deeper than the unavailability of produce and minimally processed foods. The greatest difficulty that low-income, poorly nourished people face is "not necessarily food scarcity, but a generalized and even traumatizing kind of material instability. Absolutely nothing about their lives is secure."[3]

Syncletica, to whom I introduced you early in this book, and Evagrius, whom you met in Week 4, belonged to an ancient Christian monastic generation that chose to live insecurely in the desert. A bit of bread, a handful of greens and some water might be all a monk ate in a day. It was an austere life to which some monks were poorly suited. In fantasies of abundant food, they sought a delectable escape from hard reality. Rebellious at times against the silent discipline of prayer, they ruminated on bodily catastrophes: protracted disease, drought and famine, careless doctors. Monks beset by gluttonous thoughts were less wannabe gourmands than hypochondriacs. In their daydreams, glorious meals took on narcotic properties. Images of sweet, clustered grapes, of figs the size of breasts, of lurid pomegranates, distracted them from their imaginary health scares. Add to their mental feasts a few imagined mouthfuls of crisp, convoluted walnuts and bowls of fresh milk, and the undernourished monks gorged themselves on gastronomic thoughts.

Whether in the fourth or the twenty-first century, a person who lives with chronic practical insecurity and nutritional scarcity is psychologically and spiritually vulnerable, apt to get carried away by images of the resources they lack. "Having less than you feel you need" is how Sendhil Mullainathan and Eldar Shafir, co-authors of *Scarcity*, define the condition. "Scarcity captures the mind. . . . When we experience scarcity of any kind, we become absorbed by it."[4] Predatory advertisers of drive-by Mega Meals and Super Gulps know this to be true.

Devout focus—a God-absorbed life free from material attachments, spiritual imbalance, and emotional reactivity—was the aim of desert monks' dietary fasts. They believed self-control engendered *apatheia* (meaning *equanimity* or *mindfulness*), which Evagrius described as "the health of the soul . . . not disturbed by changing events . . . unmoved at the memory of them as well."[5]

Yet Evagrius' relationship with food was by any standard unhealthy.

For fourteen of his monastic years, he abstained from eating fruit or cooked food and drank far too little water. "He ruined his digestive tract and probably suffered from urinary tract stones."[6] So determined was Evagrius to resist a food fixation that he became preoccupied with fasting.

Somewhere between the dehydrated organs of the desert monk and the insulin-resistance that obesity can cause, lies the broad, moderate range where enough is enough. Eating well in the moderate range is a matter of access, discernment, and balance, knowing what to consume, where to get it, when to start, how to quit, and whether it's sustainably, securely available. *Discernment* is rooted in the culinary word *sift*. As a sieve separates wheat from chaff, so a discerning mind tells the difference between fresh fruit and Froot Loops.

If the nearest produce vendor is a dozen miles away and you don't have a car, chances are you'll settle for sugar-laden breakfast cereals and the other starchy, processed products you can buy at the convenience mart. Therefore, my congregation's Mission Team encourages donors to our local food bank to be "protein partners" who add more canned meats than dried pastas to the public pantry's shelves. Offerings of backyard-grown citrus as well as fresh potatoes, celery, onions, and carrots are encouraged, too.

Maybe you struggle to put food on the table. Perhaps your family must rely on the charitable food boxes to which many congregations contribute. What you can do to help eradicate hunger depends in part on your material stability. If you struggle every month to make ends meet, you may have little energy left to advocate for public policy changes that would increase investment in underserved neighborhoods lacking supermarkets. Even so, collective action can multiply a little effort into a meaningful impact. For example, according to an agreed-on set of emphases, people in Presbyterian Hunger Action Congregations work together not only to end hunger but also to address its root causes. In and beyond this Lent, might you, through your church, take a little compassionate action alongside others to transform a food desert into a produce garden?

Come, Lord Jesus, be our guest.
May our meals be so blessed
we are strengthened to address

unjust hungers and unrest
neighbors not so far from here
suffer, though you, Lord, are near.
Amen.

Maundy Thursday

Whose Feet Will You Wash?

Then turning toward the woman, he said to Simon, "Do you see this woman? I entered your house; you gave me no water for my feet, but she has bathed my feet with her tears and dried them with her hair."

—Luke 7:44

You wash away the dirt I trekked through to reach you. You wash my feet with compassion, not servitude, as I have done for you. Others see and turn to me, drawn by your clearly outpoured love.

In the Republic of Türkiye, which was once called Asia Minor, we drove a rented car into Central Anatolia and came at last to the Cappadocian town of Göreme. There we'd reserved furnished lodgings in a cave. We dropped wearily, gratefully, into our underground bed. Hours later, I woke up unable to tell if it was midnight or midday. No darkness is as dark as cave darkness. Your mind can't wrap itself around darkness that deep, so it conjures up images—anything to process or seemingly perceive. I blinked and remembered a dream: my former Christian History professor was driving me home.

Lying there, unseeing, I understood. I had entered a spiritual homeland, a country of long-bygone people whose lineage was mine by faith. Here in Cappadocia, many centuries earlier, Christians had developed contemplative wisdom that I and others yet seek to know. Now my still-sleeping husband and I were sheltered by the same tuff and basalt rocks into which these, our spiritual ancestors, had carved their churches in antiquity.

After Ken woke up, we packed braided cheese, dried apricots, and bottled water to venture on foot into an arid, sculptural landscape reminiscent of the southern Arizona desert. Natural rock spires, "fairy chimneys," rose from the earth like the towering geologic hoodoos in the Chiricahua Mountains near our Tucson home. I shared our cheese with a stray dog that followed us for miles through the Valley of the Monks. We sang "Amazing Grace" in an empty cave where traces of saints' painted images remained on the walls, though religious iconoclasts had scratched away their faces.

One Cappadocian saint of the fourth century was Basil of Caesarea, a forceful monastic theologian, bishop, and advocate for social justice. Unlike some of his Christian contemporaries who lived in intentional solitude, Basil was drawn to community life. He questioned the hermit's calling: "Whose feet will you wash, whom will you look after, how can you be last of all, if you live by yourself?"[1] His words should not be taken as a criticism of single people in the present day. Basil was responding to a social and religious phenomenon of his time and place, in which many Christians believed the best way to follow Jesus was to emulate for their entire lives his forty days of desert solitude.

Basil was a servant-leader for whom human compassion signified God's activity on earth. During the dry, freezing Cappadocian winter of 368 CE, wealthy people hoarded grain, causing famine among the region's poor. With his substantial inheritance, Basil created a community meal center and established a house of healing that came to be known as the first hospital. In a blistering sermon, "To the Rich," he interrogated his socially privileged hearers: "What answer shall you make to the judge, you who dress walls, but will not clothe a man; who spruce up horses, and overlook an unfashionable brother; who leave grain to rot, but will not feed the starving; who bury your money and despise the oppressed?"[2]

If you attend a Maundy Thursday worship service today, you're unlikely to hear such an accusatory message. "Love one another" seems a likelier sermonic theme, consistent with the story of Jesus, who got up in the middle of his last supper with his disciples to wash their feet, then taught them to do the same for each other (John 13:13–17, 31b–35). Whether or not you participate in a liturgical footwashing ritual today, Basil's "Whose feet will you wash?" is a question of compassion that warrants reflection and an embodied response. Compassion is not only a tenderhearted feeling. It's more, even, than an ethical choice. At its most richly incarnate, compassion is a way of life that reverences living beings and acts to alleviate their suffering without fetishizing it.

To summarize the weeks that you and I have walked together through the Lenten desert: Compassion begins in a broken-open heart. In an outstretched hand, compassion makes a personal connection, wakefully tolerates distress, and mindfully cultivates understanding. Compassion resists the condemnatory impulse and treats with dignity and loving-kindness anyone who's suffering. The person of compassion helps and honors others but doesn't do for them the good they can do for themselves and their neighbors.

If you have come to this last day in Lent feeling you still have more to learn about compassion, take heart. Even after their intensive travels with Jesus, his disciples still needed more compassion formation. This became clear following his final supper with them. He asked them to keep vigil nearby while he prayed. But they drifted off to sleep and he wound up agonizing alone.

Let neither the disciples' avoidant drowsing nor the times you've withheld compassion cause you to despair. Start where you are, with self-compassion. Be as kind to yourself as you would be to a hurting friend who's fallen short of their spiritual potential. Trust God to see you through the night of betrayal and failure to the day of blessing and forgiveness when the world and you will be made new. Don't worry, you'll be shown whose feet to wash.

A great cloud of witnesses lives for you
amid the rocks and distances,
in songs that echo off the stones.
Saints whose bones long ago turned to dust
live for you in memory-prayers that rise
to your heart in the skies, where you dream us.
By your compassion, we become
your heart on earth,
your hand outstretched,
your love made flesh.
Amen.

Afterword

Triduum

Three Days in the Heart

"I went down to the land whose bars closed upon me forever;
yet you brought up my life from the Pit, O LORD my God."
—Jonah 2:6b

*You have just begun to learn all I have to teach you. Grave
events must occur before you can be free. You will balk and
run for what you think is your own life. Run, my beloved, but
remember, all paths lead eventually to me. When you arrive,
it will be because I journeyed with you. I'll welcome you and
offer you my life.*

"Triduum" is an ancient word that may be new to you. Borrowed from
Latin and pronounced *TRID yoo uhm*, it means *three days* and is a collective name for Maundy Thursday, Good Friday, and Holy Saturday.
At the Lord's Supper on Maundy Thursday, Lent ends, and the Triduum, "the heart of the Christian year,"[1] begins. Now that Lent has
ended, I hope you'll find a way to participate in services of worship
that lead the faithful through remembrances of Jesus' betrayal, death,
and burial. Without these consequences of his wholly self-giving life,
Easter's holy meaning can't be fully known.

Jesus anticipated his arrest, passion, and entombment, calling this
triduum "three days and three nights . . . in the heart of the earth,"
and likening it to the prophet Jonah's journey "in the belly of the sea
monster" (Matt. 12:40). Thomas Merton, the brilliant contemplative

writer of the twentieth century, whose language I have borrowed as this book's central image and title, also wrote of Jonah (or as Merton and others have called him, Jonas). In *The Sign of Jonas,* a collection of entries from his monastic journals, Merton said, "It was when Jonas was traveling as fast as he could away from Ninevah, toward Tharsis, that he was thrown overboard and swallowed by a whale who took him where God wanted him to go. . . . Even our mistakes are eloquent, more than we know."[2]

A sense of sacred irony, of eloquent mistakes, has for centuries enabled Christians to call the Friday of Jesus' torturous execution "good." This is not a matter of putting a happy spin on a grisly, unjust tragedy. Good Friday, and all Christian life, is about embracing paradox. Jesus' teachings and his death reveal sacred contradictions. The truth that you or I may try to avoid, the pain we're loath to face, point the way toward our freedom from captivating lies that perpetuate our suffering. When you and I embrace Jesus' essential paradox—that to lose is to gain and to die is to live—we come to God, who gathers up the broken pieces of the world and makes them more complete and beautiful than they were before they broke. God integrates all fractious dualities into the wholeness of life that Christians call eternal salvation. It's a life we get to live here and now, by grace and faith. It's the life toward which Lent has always pointed.

Following his jubilant entry into Jerusalem (which Christians celebrate on Palm Sunday), Jesus told his disciples, "The hour has come for the Son of Man to be glorified. Very truly, I tell you, unless a grain of wheat falls into the earth and dies, it remains just a single grain; but if it dies, it bears much fruit" (John 12:23b–24). Pay attention to that pivotal *unless* and understand: without the fatal fall, no glorious resurrected life can be lived.

From this divine paradox, it follows that there can be no compassion without passion, no responsive loving-kindness unless there first comes suffering. Until God ultimately mends all of creation's broken pieces, there will come suffering. Jesus pointed to this truth when he said, "For you always have the poor with you" (Matt. 26:11a). In the same breath, he told his disciples that the woman who had just anointed his head with precious oil (to the disciples' disapproval) had done so to prepare his body for burial. He affirmed her for embracing with costly compassion what the disciples couldn't face: the inevitability of suffering and death—Jesus' own and everyone's.

Fierce mercy, not morbidity, drove Jesus' realism. "You will know the truth," Jesus said to those who trusted him, "and the truth will make you free" (John 8:32). By his clear-eyed honesty, Jesus revealed holy, ironic wholeness. Denying pain would intensify it but facing hard facts of life and death would lead people deep into reality, the only place where God eternal can be found.

Such is the logic and the lure of the desert. Jesus relinquished all companionship, distractions, and comforts to love God alone in the unsparing wilderness. His experience there of human fragility, devilish delusion, and divine fidelity prepared him, when the time came, to emerge from the desert and share God's compassion with the world's deserted people.

The time has come for you to emerge from Lent and for me to conclude this book of devotions. In the days ahead, may you know what Thomas Merton meant when he said, "It is in the desert of compassion that the thirsty land turns into springs of water, that the poor possess all things."[3] By the overflow of God's loving-kindness, may you find you have been given all you need to live with compassion for yourself and for every living being.

Water gone stagnant in a lightless cistern,
you sweeten with mercy.
You break the cask of my fearful heart
and free me to serve the wine I've been hiding.
You transform my burdens into bread,
stone into a pillow for my head.
You grant me rest from all my striving,
then awaken me with daylight.
You clear my mind to see
the charred ruins of the world you love,
now turned wet and green, defiantly arising.
Amen.

Acknowledgments

I thank God for everyone whose gifts strengthened me as I worked to bring this book into being, especially:

Ken McAllister, the love of my life, who keeps me honest, encouraged, and laughing;

Alex Hendrickson, my multitalented BFF whose graphic design skills deserve special recognition;

Bernice Parker-Jones, Carol Reynolds, Francis Miller, John Cofield, and Sonya Green; truly Peerless Peers;

Mary Wildner-Bassett, the best *anam cara* in the West;

Arianna Gray, a wilderness guide and manuscript reader of uncommon compassion and insight;

the contemplative souls of the Shalem Institute for Spiritual Formation, especially the Going Deeper participants of 2020–2021;

the dear and faithful people of Mountain Shadows Presbyterian Church, a community of compassion in the desert;

Sheila Mahoney Keefe, the prayerful painter whose artwork graces the book's cover;

Margaret and Bill Franke of Hand Artes Gallery in Truchas, New Mexico;

Jessica Miller Kelley, a timely, keen-eyed editor, and her diligent colleagues at WJK Press, including Alison Wingfield, Natalie Smith, Michele Blum, and Julie Tonini;

the indigenous peoples of Tucson—O'odham and Yaqui—on whose desert lands I am grateful to live.

Notes

Ash Wednesday

1. Thomas Merton, *The Intimate Merton: His Life from His Journals*, ed. Patrick Hart and Jonathan Montaldo (New York: HarperCollins, 1999), 86.

First Saturday of Lent

1. George W. Hammond, "Destination Arizona: Where Are People Moving From? And Why?" *Arizona's Economy*, September 23, 2020, http://www.azeconomy.org/2020/09/economy/destination-arizona-where-are-people-moving-from-and-why/.

2. Samuel Brody, "The Characteristics, Causes, and Consequences of Sprawling Development Patterns in the United States," *The Nature Education Knowledge Project*, 2013, https://www.nature.com/scitable/knowledge/library/the-characteristics-causes-and-consequences-of-sprawling-103014747/.

3. James Goehring, "Alone in the Desert?" *Christian History Institute*, https://christianhistoryinstitute.org/magazine/article/alone-in-the-desert.

4. Pseudo-Athanasius, *The Life & Regimen of the Blessed & Holy Syncletica, Part One: The Translation*, trans. Elizabeth Bryson Bongie (Eugene, OR: Wipf and Stock Publishers, 2005), 59.

5. John Newton, "Amazing Grace, How Sweet the Sound" in Glory to God: The Presbyterian Hymnal (Louisville, KY: Westminster John Knox Press, 2013), 649.

Week 1: Remove the Heart of Stone

1. Susan Yanos, "The Midwestern Winter as Spiritual Desert," Bearings Online, December 5, 2019, https://collegevilleinstitute.org/bearings/midwest-winter-spiritual-desert/.

Tuesday of Week 1

1. R.E. Wycherley, "The Stones of Athens," *Greece and Rome* 21, no. 1 (April 1974): 54.

Thursday of Week 1

1. "Border Patrol Strategic Plan 1994 and Beyond: National Strategy," Homeland Security Digital library, July 1994, https://www.hsdl.org/?abstract&did =721845.

2. Humane Borders Fonteras Compasivas, https://humaneborders.org/our -mission/.

Friday of Week 1

1. Daniel L. Schutte, "I, the Lord of Sea and Sky," in *Glory to God: The Presbyterian Hymnal* (Louisville, KY: Westminster John Knox Press, 2013), 69.

2. Walter Burghardt, "Contemplation: A Long Loving Look at the Real," *Church Winter* (1989): 14–18.

Saturday of Week 1

1. Victoria Lemle Beckner, "The Key Skill We Rarely Learn: How to Feel Your Feelings," *Psychology Today*, October 12, 2020, https://www.psychologytoday .com/us/blog/harnessing-principles-change/202010/the-key-skill-we-rarely-learn -how-feel-your-feelings.

2. Beckner, "Key Skill."

Week 2: Reach Out Your Hand

1. John O'Donohue, "Introduction," *To Bless the Space Between Us: A Book of Blessings* (New York: Doubleday, 2008), xv.

Monday of Week 2

1. "What is Compassion?" *Greater Good Magazine*, https://greatergood .berkeley.edu/topic/compassion/definition#what_is.

Tuesday of Week 2

1. Christopher Conover, "'Stupid Motorist Law' Rarely Enforced in Tucson Area," *Arizona Public Media*, September 11, 2019, https://news.azpm.org/p/news -topical-nature/2019/9/11/157986-stupid-motorist-law-rarely-enforced-in-tucson -area/.

2 . Brian J. Pedersen, "Stupid Motorist Law, Extreme Parent Ignorance Edition," *Tucson Weekly*, September 11, 2012, https://www.tucsonweekly.com /TheRange/archives/2012/09/11/stupid-motorist-law-extreme-parent-ignorance -edition.

Thursday of Week 2

1. Derek Thompson, "Workism is Making Americans Miserable," *The Atlantic*, February 24, 2019, https://www.theatlantic.com/ideas/archive/2019/02/religion -workism-making-americans-miserable/583441/.

Saturday of Week 2

1. Jeanne Stevenson-Moessner, "How Dying Churches Abuse Pastors," *The Christian Century*, April 23, 2020, https://www.christiancentury.org/review/books/how-dying-churches-abuse-pastors.

2. Henry Cloud and John Townsend, "When Someone Responds to Your Boundaries with Anger," *Boundaries* (blog), February 14, 2022, https://www.boundariesbooks.com/blogs/boundaries-blog-when-someone-responds-to-your-boundaries-with-anger.

Week 3: Stay Awake with Me

1. Henri J. M. Nouwen, *The Wounded Healer: Ministry in Contemporary Society* (New York: Doubleday, 1972), 72.

Tuesday of Week 3

1. John Fawcett, "Blest Be the Tie That Binds" in *Glory to God: The Presbyterian Hymnal* (Louisville, KY: Westminster John Knox Press, 2013), 306.

Wednesday of Week 3

1. Marsha Linehan, "Distress Tolerance: Crisis Survival, Radical Acceptance, and Addiction Skills," April 14, 2017, https://www.youtube.com/watch?v=Za2nTuGJJAI.

2. Jillian Glasgow, "A Daily Dose of Dialectics," *Broadview Psychology* (blog), May 11, 2020, http://broadviewpsychology.com/2020/05/11/a-daily-dose-of-dialectics/.

Thursday of Week 3

1. "Mulberry Tree and Olive Tree Control," Pima County Ord. 1991-137 § 19 (part), 1991, https://codelibrary.amlegal.com/codes/pimacounty/latest/pimacounty_az/0-0-0-3069.

2. Mort Rosenblum, "It's Time to End the Pima County Ban on Olive Trees," *Arizona Daily Star*, September 26, 2021, https://tucson.com/opinion/local/mort-rosenblum-its-time-to-end-the-pima-county-ban-on-olie-trees/article_d3b25a0e-06a9-11ec-9f78-1bc9ed83d57a.html.

3. Don Page, Review, Garden of Gethsemane, *Yelp*, October 24, 2021, https://www.yelp.com/user_details?userid=VwGK-O1oFqulWqiMxu7i-w.

4. James Montgomery, "Go to Dark Gethsemane" in *Glory to God: The Presbyterian Hymnal* (Louisville, KY: Westminster John Knox Press, 2013), 220.

Friday of Week 3

1. Trisha Dowling, "Compassion Does Not Fatigue!" *The Canadian Veterinary Journal* 59, no. 7 (July 2018), https://pubmed.ncbi.nlm.nih.gov/30026620/.

2. Dowling, "Compassion."

3. Definition of *compassion fatigue*, *Merriam-Webster Dictionary*, https://www.merriam-webster.com/dictionary/compassion%20fatigue.

4. Dowling, "Compassion."

Saturday of Week 3

1. Eugene H. Peterson, *The Message: The Bible in Contemporary Language* (Colorado Springs: NavPress Publishing Group, 2003), 1666.

2. Andrew Dreitcer, *Living Compassion: Loving Like Jesus* (Nashville: Upper Room Books, 2017), 16.

3. Dreitcer, *Living Compassion*, 16.

4. "Lord, Make Us More Holy," *Glory to God: The Presbyterian Hymnal* (Louisville, KY: Westminster John Knox Press, 2013), 313.

5. https://compassioncenter.arizona.edu/about.

6. Tania Singer and Olga M. Klimecki, "Empathy and Compassion," *Current Biology*, vol. 24, no. 18 (September 22, 2014), https://www.sciencedirect.com/search?qs=compassion&pub=Current%20Biology&cid=272099.

7. Michael Dowling, "Customised Altruism and Compassion Meditation," March 21, 2017, https://blackwooduc.org.au/downloads/resources-for-personal-exploration/guided-compassion-meditation/.

Monday of Week 4

1. Evagrius Ponticus, "The 153 Chapters on Prayer" in *The Praktikos— Chapters on Prayer*, trans. John Eudes Bamberger, OCSO (Spencer, MA: Cistercian Publications, 1972), 65.

2. Palladius of Aspuna, in "Evagrius Ponticus" in *The Lausiac History*, trans. John Wortley (Collegeville, MN: Liturgical Press, 2015), 95.

Tuesday of Week 4

1. Evagrius Ponticus, "The Hundred Chapters," in *The Praktikos—Chapters on Prayer*, trans. John Eudes Bamberger, OCSO (Spencer, MA: Cistercian Publications, 1972), 21.

2. "MLK: A Riot Is the Language of the Unheard," *Sixty Minutes Overtime*, August 25, 2013, https://www.cbsnews.com/news/mlk-a-riot-is-the-language-of-the-unheard/.

3. Gail Strange, "We Must Go Beyond the One-Day Worship Service," *Presbyterian News Service*, January 28, 2022, https://www.presbyterianmission.org/story/we-must-go-beyond-the-one-day-worship-service/.

4. Evagrius Ponticus, "The Hundred Chapters," *The Praktikos—Chapters on Prayer*, trans. John Eudes Bamberger, OCSO (Spencer, MA: Cistercian Publications, 1972), 36–37.

5. Matteo Fagotto, "The Monk Who Saves Manuscripts from ISIS," *The Atlantic*, February 23, 2017, https://www.theatlantic.com/international/archive/2017/02/the-monk-who-saves-manuscripts-from-isis/517611/.

Thursday of Week 4

1. "Meditative Singing," *At the Wellspring of Faith*, July 27, 2004, https://www.taize.fr/en_article338.html.

2. Frederic and Mary Ann Brussat, "Brother Roger of Taize," *Spirituality & Practice*, https://www.spiritualityandpractice.com/book-reviews/view/15956/brother-roger-of-taize.

3. J. Whitgift, "The Priory Church of Reconciliation," http://wikimapia.org/19734259/The-Priory-Church-of-Reconciliation.

4. Barbara Bradley Hagerty, "Prayer May Reshape Your Brain . . . and Your Reality," *All Things Considered*, May 20, 2009, https://www.npr.org/templates/story/story.php?storyId=104310443.

5. "Brother Roger's Unfinished Letter," *At the Wellspring of Faith*, December 12, 2005, https://www.taize.fr/en_article2964.html.

Saturday of Week 4

1. Paul Gilbert, "Training Our Minds in, with, and for Compassion," 2010, https://www.getselfhelp.co.uk/docs/GILBERT-COMPASSION-HANDOUT.pdf.

Monday of Week 5

1. Charles Haddon Spurgeon, "Means for Restoring the Banished," *Metropolitan Tabernacle Pulpit*, vol. 16, September 11, 1870, https://www.spurgeon.org/resource-library/sermons/means-for-restoring-the-banished/#flipbook/.

2. "Brief Statement of Faith," *Presbyterian Church (U.S.A.)*, https://www.presbyterianmission.org/what-we-believe/brief-statement-of-faith/.

3. John J. Moment, "God of Compassion, in Mercy Befriend Us" in *Glory to God: The Presbyterian Hymnal* (Louisville, KY: Westminster John Knox Press, 2013), 436.

Tuesday of Week 5

1. Dietrich Bonhoeffer, *London, 1933–1935: Works, Volume 13*, ed. Keith Celements, trans. Isabel Best (Minneapolis: Fortress, 2007), 40.

2. Dietrich Bonhoeffer, *The Cost of Discipleship* (New York: Touchstone, 1995), 215–16.

Wednesday of Week 5

1. John Watson, *The Homely Virtues* (London: Hodder & Stoughton, 1903), 168.

Friday of Week 5

1. "What Barna's New Data Says About the Perception of Church," *Church Fuel* (blog), https://churchfuel.com/what-barnas-new-data-says-about-the-perception-of-church/.

2. Paul Gilbert, "The Origins and Nature of Compassion Focused Therapy," *British Journal of Clinical Psychology* 53, 2014, 6.

Saturday of Week 5

1. "Women's Rights," Human Rights Watch World Report 2001, https://www.hrw.org/legacy/press/2001/04/un_oral12_0405.htm.

2. Ayaan Hirsi Ali, "Honor Killings in America," *The Atlantic*, April 30, 2015, https://www.theatlantic.com/politics/archive/2015/04/honor-killings-in-america/391760/.

Holy Week: Do This and You Will Live

1. "Quotes on Judaism & Israel: Rabbi Hillel," Babylonian Talmud, Shabbat 31a, *Jewish Virtual Library*, https://www.jewishvirtuallibrary.org/rabbi-hillel-quotes-on-judaism-and-israel.

Monday of Holy Week

1. Fyodor Dostoevsky, *The Idiot*, trans. Richard Pevear and Larissa Volokhonsky (New York: Vintage, 2003).

Tuesday of Holy Week

1. David Gambrell, "Lord, to You Our People Cry," Presbyterian Mission Agency, 2015, http://pma.pcusa.org/site_media/media/uploads/worship/pdfs/lord,_to_you_our_people_cry.pdf.

Wednesday of Holy Week

1. Shirin McArthur, "Living in a Food Desert," *Shirin McArthur* (blog), August 20, 2017, https://shirinmcarthur.com/2017/08/20/living-in-a-food-desert/.

2. Heather Tirado Gilligan, "Food Deserts Aren't the Problem," *Slate*, February 10, 2014, http://www.slate.com/articles/life/food/2014/02/food_deserts_and_fresh_food_access_aren_t_the_problem_poverty_not_obesity.html.

3. James McWilliams, "Why Are So Many Low Income People So Overweight?" *Pacific Standard*, August 4, 2014, http://www.psmag.com/health-and-behavior/many-low-income-people-overweight-87379.

4. Sendhil Mullainathan, Eldar Shafir, *Scarcity: Why Having Too Little Means So Much*, (New York: Henry Holt, 2013), 7.

5. Evagrius Ponticus, *The Praktikos & Chapters on Prayer*, trans. John Eudes Bamberger, OCSO (Spencer, MA: Cistercian Publications), 56, 67.

6. Augustine Casiday, ed., *Evagrius Ponticus* (New York: Routledge, 2006), 13.

Maundy Thursday

1. St. Basil, *Solitude and Communion, Papers on the Hermit Life*, ed. A.M. Allchin (Oxford: SLG Press, 1977), 30–47.

2. St. Basil, "Sermon to the Rich," trans. Peter Gilbert, *De Unione Ecclisiarum* (blog), October 25, 2008, https://bekkos.wordpress.com/st-basils-sermon-to-the-rich/.

Afterword

1. Emily Enders Odom, "Reclaiming Triduum: The Great Three Days," *Presbyterian Mission Agency,* March 15, 2016, https://www.pcusa.org/news/2016/3/15/reclaiming-triduum-great-three-days/.

2. Thomas Merton, *The Sign of Jonas* (New York: Harcourt, Brace, 1953), 10–11.

3. Thomas Merton, *The Intimate Merton: His Life from His Journals*, ed. Patrick Hart, Jonathan Montaldo (New York: HarperCollins, 1999), 86.

CPSIA information can be obtained
at www.ICGtesting.com
Printed in the USA
LVHW012001041222
734501LV00002B/2